The

with The Ac

The Worlds is set in modern times. It contrasts factory strikes, a businessman's take-over and terrorist kidnappings. Its cast ranges from those who sit in the cabinet to those who work on the shop floor, from a chief policeman to terrorists on the run. It looks at the moral basis of our social life, asks 'Who are the greatest terrorists?' and gives a disturbing answer.

Also included in this volume are *The Activists Papers*, an extensive collection of essays, poems, stories and statements written by Bond while he was directing the play. In them he examines basic questions of culture in both the narrow and broad sense – and looks at the future not only of literature but of ourselves.

by the same author

in Methuen's Modern Plays

SAVED
NARROW ROAD TO THE DEEP NORTH
THE POPE'S WEDDING
LEAR
THE SEA
BINGO
THE FOOL and WE COME TO THE RIVER
THE BUNDLE
THE WOMAN

in Methuen's New Theatrescripts

A-A-AMERICA! and STONE

in the Master Playwrights series

PLAYS: ONE (The Pope's Wedding, Saved, Early Morning)
PLAYS: TWO (Lear, The Sea, Narrow Road to the Deep North,
Black Mass *and* Passion)

also available

THEATRE POEMS AND SONGS

Edward Bond

THE WORLDS

with The Activists Papers

EYRE METHUEN
LONDON

First published 1980 by Eyre Methuen Ltd
11 New Fetter Lane, London EC4P 4EE
Copyright © 1980 by Edward Bond
Set, printed and bound in Great Britain by
Fakenham Press Limited, Fakenham, Norfolk

ISBN 0 413 46600 0 (*Hardback*)
ISBN 0 413 46610 8 (*Paperback*)

CAST

TRENCH
HUBBARD
KENDAL
HARRIS
TERRY
RAY
JOHN
LORD BIGDYKE
POLICE CHIEF
GATE
BARWAY
MICHAEL
THE PERFECT WAITER
WHITE FIGURE
ANNA
LISA
BERYL
MARIAN
SYLVIA
PRU
LOUISE LINNELL
TWO VOICES (off), one man and one woman

LIST OF SCENES

NOTE
Some of the speeches in this play have titles. These are
not to be spoken by the actors. They are intended to be
a guide to interpretation.

E.B.

The Worlds was first performed by Newcastle University Theatre Society at the Newcastle Playhouse on 8th March 1979 with the following cast:

TRENCH	Graham Blockey
HUBBARD	Andrew O'Hanlon
KENDAL	Ken Price
HARRIS	Steve Bolam
TERRY	Dave Spear
RAY	Tony Dunn
JOHN	Harry Nodwell
LORD BIGDYKE	James Carpmale
POLICE CHIEF	Owen Aaronovitch
GATE	Guy Holmes
BARWAY	Tim Wyatt
MICHAEL	James Nuttgens
THE PERFECT WAITER	Brian Farrell
WHITE FIGURE	Tim Wyatt
ANNA	Louise Kerr
LISA	Alison Southern
BERYL	Nicola Rotsos
MARIAN	Peta Hoult
SYLVIA	Vicki Bennison
PRU	Caroline Hall
LOUISE LINNELL	Debbie Bestwick
JOAN	Sarah Smith

Directed by Edward Bond (*assisted by* Peter Biddle)
Designed by Hayden Griffin and Eamon D'Arcy
Lighting by Andy Phillips (*assisted by* Lolly Schenck)
Scenic artist Dave Lawes; *Production Assistant* Craig Dickson;
Set construction Phillip Bailey; *Properties* Alix Gibson;
Sound Dave Cross; *Wardrobe* Kim Ridley

The Worlds was also presented by The Activists Youth Theatre Club at The Royal Court Theatre Upstairs, London on 21st November 1979 with the following cast:

TRENCH	Geoff Church
HUBBARD	Lindsay Joe Wesker
KENDAL	Mark French
HARRIS	Tom Hodgkins
TERRY	Dan Hildebrand
RAY	Gordon Warren
JOHN	Dave Toneri
LORD BIGDYKE	Bart Peel
POLICE CHIEF	Matthew Purves
GATE	Peter Watson
MICHAEL	Peter Malan
WHITE FIGURE	Patrick Bailey
ANNA	Julie Wallace
LISA	Faith Tingle
BERYL	Belinda Blanchard
MARIAN	Jessica Hawkesly
SYLVIA	Fiona McAlpine
PRU	Diana Judd
LOUISE LINNELL	Caroline Cook

Directed by Edward Bond (*assisted by* Peter Cox)
Designed by Eamon D'arcy
Lighting by Andy Phillips
Sound Peter Deacon
Stage Manager Matthew Richardson (*assisted by* Rebecca Madron, Meganne Hover, Lucy Hornak, Tom Moeschinger

Two changes in the cast were made for this production. The artist BARWAY was not cast. His 'presence' was created by the reactions of the actors. His line on page 14 was spoken by HUBBARD. His lines on page 16 were cut. THE PERFECT WAITER and MICHAEL were made the same person.

Part One

ONE

Country Hotel
TRENCH *in an armchair.* HUBBARD, KENDAL *and* HARRIS *stand round him.* BARWAY *sketches.*

TRENCH. When the war ended I came out of the army with a scar, a demob suit with a few quid in the pocket and a lot of experience of life and men rammed into six years. I invested that and a lot of hard work and long hours. The result: TCC. It's not all due to me. I know what I owe the team. Some of us have been together for a long time. Some of us are newer comers. But we can all call ourself one of the team.

REST. Here here.

TRENCH *(toast)*. To thirty years.

REST. Thirty years.

HUBBARD *(toasting)*. And to you JT for the –

KENDAL. Great meal JT.

HARRIS. Well JT at dinner you talked of experience –

KENDAL. Excellent salmon.

HARRIS. – and determination. Right. And I'm not afraid of mentioning a few more old-fashioned virtues. Such as guts. Go out and get it. Self-help. Young people ask for adventure. Well running our organization is adventure!

TRENCH. It is.

HARRIS. Goodlor! Leading four thousand men. Understanding their motivation. Being father. Friend. Disciplinarian when need be. Holding the crew on –

TRENCH. Indeed. We don't often get a chance to talk like this. That's wrong. Job can't be done if you lose the long

view. Now you say the young. What about Kendal's boys?
If I had lads I'd've hoped they turned out like them. If I
have my way they're coming into the team. Mind they'll
have to prove themselves.

KENDAL. They're keen to do it JT.

HARRIS. Yes Ken's lads are turning out just like their father.

TRENCH. Ronnie's right: a changing world. And we're part
of the change. America was there before Columbus discovered it. But we're *making* a new world. Those who have
the stuff of the builder in them.

HUBBARD (*toasting*). And to you JT for the –

KENDAL. Wait a mo Jimmy. I'd like to hear JT on that.

TRENCH. Stuff of the builder?

KENDAL. What is that?

TRENCH (*puffs cheeks, then*): Phoo ... well.

KENDAL. One part intelligence to two parts character and a
squeeze of recklessness shaken up with a lot of experience.

> HUBBARD *retires to one side. The bottle dangles from his
> hand. He tries to stay awake.*

TRENCH. What is character?

HARRIS. Ah there we are.

TRENCH. We can measure intelligence. But how to measure
character? That is the question. Well it's a country
weekend so let's play a game. I ask my think tank: what is
character?

HARRIS (*Looks at* KENDAL). We all know what it is.

KENDAL. But how to define it.

HARRIS. Pon my word yes.

HUBBARD. Ickle more vino? (*He fills his glass.*)

KENDAL. The way a chap looks at you. And the handshake.

TRENCH. Hm. Could be con tricks.

KENDAL. O I don't know JT.

HARRIS. I agree with JT. Sorry.

KENDAL. You can train yourself to spot the creepy-crawlies.

HUBBARD. Do a market survey.

HARRIS. Life. You see if a man fails that.

TRENCH. Mm. Young fella out of college comes in your office. Calls you sir. Looks you in the eye. Why not? – he doesn't know the problem. Firm handshake? – could be brazen. Will it shake when he puts it in the till? And you can't tell if he's failed in life because he hasn't lived it.

HARRIS. Spot on JT.

HUBBARD. Put us out of our misery.

TRENCH. You chaps have all got it. It's the whole man.

HARRIS. Ah now ... that is clever ... the whole man.

TRENCH. He respects and judges you as he does himself. What you invest in a man is what you get out of him. Yes, at times we do harsh things. But we do it cleanly. For the good of the customer. With no malice. No pleasure. We push a man overboard and we sail on. But we throw a lifebelt in the sea behind us. We're all brothers. Big brothers and little brothers. As in every family. At the end of the day we can all offer the next man our hand. Be he from the shop floor or the directors' suite. Couldn't do the job if I didn't believe that.

KENDAL. O it's rewarding to have these talks.

TRENCH. I don't apologize for saying that.

KENDAL. My god what an age when you have to apologize for being profound!

TRENCH. Well now. You may have noticed a little man.

KENDAL. Ha ha.

TRENCH. No doubt you're wondering who he is.

HARRIS. One of JT's little surprises.

HUBBARD. Thought you'd wined us so well I was seeing things.

TRENCH. And what he's scribbling on his pad.

KENDAL. Ha ha. Tax inspector.

TRENCH (*snap*). Artist.

KENDAL (*defensive*). Well they all wear long hair these days.

TRENCH. I'm marking our thirty years with a portrait.

HARRIS. O splendid.

KENDAL. And generous JT. Painter laddies don't come cheap.

TRENCH. Mind not a portrait of me. The team.

HARRIS. Ah now.

TRENCH. Don't want me scowling down at you from the wall as well as from the top of the table.

KENDAL. A handsome gesture.

TRENCH. Thought I'd do it.

BARWAY. Head up a shade.

KENDAL. Sorry old man. My wife's mother paints.

HARRIS. You amaze me JT.

TRENCH. Say why Ronnie.

HARRIS. For two weeks the organization's been paralysed by strike. Thirty per cent demand. No sign of breakthrough. And you invite us away for a pleasant weekend in a fine country hotel in beautiful grounds as your personal guests. You've had a gruelling week and a long drive down. And you sit there and discuss art and life. And you make sense.

TRENCH. We're funny people.

KENDAL. My god I wish there were a few more of us. JT you know me well enough for me to say this and not be mis-understood.

HUBBARD (*to himself*). Might as well empty the bottle. Insult to waste wine of this calibre. (*He pours himself a drink.*)

KENDAL. Anyway it ought to be said. Neck out then. If we're being philosophical – and there's no harm in that when it's past midnight as long as you don't make it a habit – then I'll *be* philosophical. It might not be Spinoza but it's worth a thought. How d'you judge a chap? You said JT: not from the eyes. You're right JT. You're not often not. But I put this question: how does a chap judge himself?

HUBBARD (*to himself*). First class vino.

TRENCH. Have I got that right?

KENDAL. How d'you look into your own eyes so to speak? (*Shrugs.*) I don't know the answer to that one. But you gave me a clue JT. Let it drop quite casually. Probably didn't even notice the significance it would have for us young ones. Trust. Yes, trust. You threw the word at us: trust. I jumped on that.

HUBBARD. Ready for shut-eye JT?

TRENCH. No this is interesting. Ken?

KENDAL (*panicking*). Well. As I say. I'm no Spinoza.

TRENCH. We're all friends here.

KENDAL (*floundering*). What-say we reformulate it like this: you have to take yourself on trust before you can trust yourself.

HUBBARD. Don't paint me holding the bottle.

KENDAL. How else can those four thousand men trust *you*? They can tell. (*Reassured at suddenly finding safe ground.*) By jimminy yes. You can't lie on the shop floor. That place is sacred.

HUBBARD. I trust you Ken.

KENDAL. Thankyou Hub. And I trust myself when I tell JT – and this is my philosophical remark: JT I'm a better man for knowing you. O there'll be sneerers. And others will say you don't say these things.

HARRIS. Well you've said it.

TRENCH. And I'm grateful.

KENDAL (*quiet malice*). What Ronnie calls the organization's worst moment – it's not for me to second that (who's to know the struggles of your early years?) but let's say: a nasty corner – and you calmly talk such wisdom. My god.

TRENCH. Now now.

KENDAL. I'm glad I said it.

TRENCH. No more thanks. It's past you youngsters' bed-time. Leave us old ones to bore ourselves to sleep.

KENDAL. Night JT. Godbless.

HARRIS. Night JT. And you Jimmy. Sleep well.

HUBBARD. Nighty-o.

> TRENCH *raises a hand in benediction.* KENDAL *and* HARRIS *go.*

TRENCH. Did you get your doodles Mr Barway?

BARWAY. One or two.

TRENCH. Catch their character. That'll prove if you're an artist. They're good lads: I almost look on them as sons. I await the masterpiece. (*He waves* BARWAY *goodnight.*) Goodnight.

BARWAY. Goodnight Mr Trench. Mr Hubbard.

> BARWAY *goes.*

An Advertisement

TRENCH. A running stream. A sky of piercing blue. No cloud. Grass and heather dry in the wind. Crisp. The water. Fish leaping well. It would be nice. To spend the days like that. They get less. (HUBBARD *snorts.*) Despatch box sent down to the lodge. Drop into the office now and then. A day in town. Drop in the club. Give you the benefit of my experience. The hot line always by my hand.

*

HUBBARD. If you don't mind I'll turn in.

A Menu

TRENCH. Fancy a walk in the morning? Come back to bacon, eggs, sausages, mushrooms, toast, rolls, butter, marmalade, fresh orange juice, coffee or tea. They do a first class kedgeree. Early morning walk take years off you. Come back like school boys. The views! Magnificence. You catch your breath.

*

HUBBARD. If I wake up. Shall I order your night cap?

TRENCH. Please. I'll expect you early. I've brought some papers for you to vet. As I'm paying for the weekend.

HUBBARD. Night then.

> HUBBARD *goes.* TRENCH *picks up a book of poems. He reads.* THE PERFECT WAITER *comes in. He carries a whisky and a bottle of soda on a silver tray.*

THE PERFECT WAITER. Goodevening sir.

TRENCH. You didn't know managing directors read poetry.

THE PERFECT WAITER. It's very nice to see sir. Shall I pour the soda sir?

TRENCH (*reading*). If you'd be so kind.

> THE PERFECT WAITER *pours. Hands the drink to* TRENCH. *Picks up the empty wine glass from beside his chair.*

THE PERFECT WAITER. Will that be all sir? (TRENCH *nods.*) Goodnight sir.

> THE PERFECT WAITER *goes.* TRENCH *drinks the whisky in two gulps. Closes the book. Lets it fall to the floor. Collapses.* THE PERFECT WAITER *comes back.*

THE PERFECT WAITER. You called sir?

> THE PERFECT WAITER *goes to* TRENCH, *looks at him and goes out. His face remains set in* THE PERFECT WAITER's *expression.* LISA *and* MICHAEL *come in. They carry guns. Their faces are hidden under balaclavas.* MICHAEL *gives his gun to* LISA. *He puts* TRENCH *across his shoulder.* LISA *keeps watch. They move towards the door.* THE PERFECT WAITER *comes back.*

THE PERFECT WAITER (*politely*). The service lift.

> THE PERFECT WAITER *goes.* LISA *and* MICHAEL *go out the other way.*

TWO

Boardroom.

HUBBARD, KENDAL, POLICE CHIEF, LORD BIGDYKE.

HARRIS. How long will it take to find him?

POLICE CHIEF. Good question.

KENDAL. Haven't you any idea?

POLICE CHIEF. Always got ideas. How will your strikers react?

HUBBARD. They're meeting tomorrow.

HARRIS. To think we'd been sitting with him then out of the blue . . .

POLICE CHIEF (*smiling*). If we do find him that's the easier part.

HUBBARD. I take over in the chairman's absence. The first question is: do we have any choice?

BIGDYKE. You have the usual obligations of rational people.

HUBBARD. I'm a businessman, I don't know what that means. Look, our concern is the organization. There's money – but we have to invest for expansion. If we cough up our profitability would take a nasty dent. The chairman or the company? What would he want us to do (*To* KENDAL *and* HARRIS:) – provided he was in a position to give an unbiased verdict.

BIGDYKE. It's natural that you see it from a limited horizon. (*He takes a sheet from his briefcase.*) I've had this from the home secretary. (*He gives the sheet to* KENDAL *who reads it.*) Suppose you're lucky. The strikers are appalled and go back on your terms. The terrorists could still hold him for ransom in the so-to-speak normal way. You say you must consider the good of your company. Fine. But there is another good. The good of society. If you give way you set a precedent. What happens at your next strike? The taking of hostages is a very primitive way of running our affairs. Everyone ought to agree on that. We're almost hardened to terrorism by nationalists, for gain by common criminals, by political groups out to demoralize and weaken government for their minority ends –

KENDAL *passes the sheet to* HUBBARD. HUBBARD *reads*.

BIGDYKE. – but this is new. Terrorists have abducted the head of a major company while it's on strike. Unless the striker's demands are met he'll be shot. Where does this lead? Suppose your football team had to play a vital match. You kidnap the Chairman of the opponent club or his child (the imagination runs on) and threaten to kill him if his side wins. Imagine the spectators at such a game. In one blow we'd be back in the arena in Rome.

KENDAL *passes the sheet to* HARRIS. HARRIS *reads*.

BIGDYKE. Or you object to the siting of a motorway. A power station. A factory. A school. A garage. A dog kennel. Civilization is built on the finding of substitutes for violence in the conduct of human affairs. The shadow of violence is very dark: it falls and engulfs everything. There is your obligation: to society.

Unnoticed by the others the POLICE CHIEF *takes the sheet from* HARRIS. *He reads it.*

BIGDYKE. You tell me that fortunately it is the same as your obligation to your organization. So be it. Don't give way. The deadline of three days will be extended. They always are. We must give the police time to locate them – and then be firm and adroit enough to free Mr Trench unscathed. Meanwhile I suggest you meet the strikers and persuade them that their obligations to the country, their employers and themselves are also in this matter – fortunately – the same. You see the Minister's concern. (*He looks for the*

Minister's letter. The POLICE CHIEF *gives it to him.*) We meet here at three tomorrow. Gentlemen.

POLICE CHIEF. I'll keep you posted. Morning.

OTHERS. Goodmorning.

LORD BIGDYKE *and the* POLICE CHIEF *go.* HUBBARD *pours himself a drink.*

HUBBARD. Anyone?

HARRIS. I will.

HUBBARD *pours. He and* HARRIS *drink.*

HARRIS. What'll the strike negotiators do?

HUBBARD. Roll like pigs in treacle.

HARRIS. Why us?

KENDAL. For god's sake Harris!

HARRIS. Why us? I can't get over the –

HUBBARD. Stop squabbling the bloody pair of you. Be grateful for the godsend.

HARRIS (*avoiding the subject*). Tomorrow's negotiations. Let's settle our line.

KENDAL. They'll say the kidnapping's irrelevant. That lot'll be sorry it wasn't all of us.

HARRIS. I think we should make a gesture. Seven percent. We'll have to in the end. It's like playing whist at a funeral parlour.

KENDAL. No way! You heard Lord Bigdyke. We stand firm.

HUBBARD. Harris thinks you stop the dog biting your leg by giving it your arm. If no one else is going to talk about it I am.

HARRIS. You want him dead.

HUBBARD (*pleasantly*). I'm not answering that Harris. It happens to be irrelevant. You know what's what. Trench blocked expansion for years. As long as we got a profit he wagged his tail. The *real* fat – he didn't let us go after that. In our business you expand or drop out. We're sitting comfortably on our arses and soon the chair's going to collapse under us. We need major new investment. There's only one answer: we go public. Put the company on the stock exchange.

HARRIS. All right! But there are some decencies! You don't haggle with the undertaker at the graveside. (*Calms down.*) It can be discussed tomorrow.

HARRIS *goes out.*

KENDAL. What's the use of saying all that to Harris? You know he likes to arrive at the accident after the blood's been spilt. The vampire with clean fangs.

HUBBARD. Exploit the situation: that's what it's about. They'll let JT go just to get him off their tits. If we let this slip away we deserve our bloody dicks chopped off. I waited for it. I hope he's shit scared and I'd like the pleasure of smelling his shit.

KENDAL. Hardly generous.

HUBBARD. Shouldn't read poetry.

THREE

Derelict House.
Empty. ANNA, LISA *and* MICHAEL *carry in* TRENCH. *They also bring camping equipment, supplies and arms. Their faces are hidden under balaclavas. They put* TRENCH *on the floor.* LISA *stands guard at the window.* ANNA *unpacks.*

MICHAEL. Is he alive?

ANNA. Tea.

MICHAEL. Price goes down if they're dead.

ANNA. Dying for a cup.

MICHAEL (*going off*). Always wanted to live in the country.

ANNA. Trench.

TRENCH. Are you going to kill me?

ANNA. Not till you've recorded this message. (*Hands him a sheet of paper.*) Are you listening? Read it first.

A Confused Reading of an Ultimatum

TRENCH (*reads. He is confused*). This is John Trench. I'm being held by RRA. I will be released when the demands of the TCC workers are met in full. If they are not met by 8 a.m. on Thursday I will be executed. Further hostages will be taken from management until the striker's demands are met. If this RRA unit is discovered other units will take hostages as necessary.

MICHAEL *comes in.*

MICHAEL. Kettle's on. Lisa?

LISA. What?

MICHAEL. We made it. We made it.

LISA. We made it. We made it.

MICHAEL *and* LISA *play a game. They hug each other, rock, laugh and repeat 'We made it', 'Lisa', 'Stop it', 'Come on', etc. – at first quietly and then gradually louder.* TRENCH *reads through it.*

ANNA. They'll be coming for the tape. (*To* TRENCH.) Faster.

TRENCH *reads.* MICHAEL *goes out.*

TRENCH. This is why RRA have taken their action. Many of the needs of human beings can now be met in industry. And science have made a sane and contented world. Possible yet it becomes increasingly irrational resources are wasted and poorer countries. Plundered while their people starve people. Are forced to seek their own ends. Without regard for the common good human relations. Are destroyed organization breaks down western society no. Longer works as it becomes increasingly irrational so it – (TRENCH *stops*.) The typing. (*Reads*.) – becomes more violent the working class cannot fit into an irrational society nor can it be coerced into fitting into it. By education inducement force. Or fear it is not enough to say this we must. Say why the working class becomes what it is through the very activity of its work that is. How its characteristic behaviour and opinions are formed clearly this cannot be. Changed the alternative is as. Clear society must be changed the working class must. Control not only production and distribution but also information and education only the working class can. Develop our wasting humanity and make society rational it has created. The physical structure of society now it must create. Its culture ... (*He stops reading*.) The words.

> As TRENCH *reads* ANNA *has gone out. She returns before he finishes reading.*

LISA. Go on.

TRENCH (*reads*). We cannot patiently wait. For society to fall apart reaction armed. With modern technology could make the end of this century a graveyard that is why. We have taken this action modern strikes create. Great tensions they are a seedbed. Of revolution we can therefore expect restrictions to be placed on them this will increase. Conflict once again. It will be shown that the relationships between classes are based. On violence therefore we fight. (*He stops reading. Bewildered*.) The words.

ANNA. Go on.

TRENCH (*reads*). I apologize to my workers for the way I have exploited them. It is my wish that as a small compensation their demands be met in full.

*

MICHAEL has come back. He switches on the tape recorder.
He gestures to TRENCH *to start. Silence.*

MICHAEL (*switches off the machine. Repeats the opening of the*
ultimatum). This is John Trench. (*He switches on the*
machine.)

TRENCH. This is John Trench. I'm being held by hooligans.
Don't give way to –

MICHAEL switches off the tape recorder.

ANNA. God you're stupid.
MICHAEL. Try again.

MICHAEL winds the tape back. He starts it again.

TRENCH. This is John Trench. Somewhere in the country.
Derelict house.

MICHAEL stops the tape recorder.

ANNA. Take the pictures.

They put TRENCH *against a wall.* MICHAEL *puts*
a placard round TRENCH's *neck. He takes flashlight*
snaps.

MICHAEL (*snapping*). Wanted to let the workers hear *you*
sweat. Give them a treat. Wouldn't expect you to treat
them.
TRENCH. I was killing at your age. In the army. I don't know
how many. I killed for what I thought was right –
MICHAEL (*kicks* TRENCH). Shut it.
TRENCH. Why d'you do this? You've got everything you
want. You don't know what poverty –
ANNA. The last argument of the philistine: I'm all right.
D'you measure everything by the trough?

MICHAEL starts to gag TRENCH.

ANNA. No let him go on. The bourgeois whimper as their world ends.

TRENCH. If you use violence others use it. We can't make these decisions. Society decides.

LISA. Fine if you're society.

MICHAEL. Kettle's on!

MICHAEL *goes*.

TRENCH. TCC won't capitulate. I don't want it.

ANNA. Courage is a vice when you use it in the wrong cause. Nothing you do or say has any value now. Go on, try again.

TRENCH (*trying to explain*). You should be helping to run the world. Not pull it apart. You must have reasons for what you do. Then explain them. Make us listen.

ANNA. We just explained. You read it.

TRENCH. But those – words.

ANNA. Meant nothing to you. This society *can't* explain itself to itself. You understand nothing. Yet the public means of explanation – press, television, theatres, courts, schools, universities – almost everywhere ideas are formed or information is collected is owned in one way or another by people like you. Even our language is owned by you. We have to learn a new language. Even our morals. We have to be different people. You think you can live half your life by the laws of banking and the other half by truth. No. Think! – in a scientific age the last thing most people know anything about is their own life.

LISA. Motorbike.

ANNA *and* LISA *remove their safety catches*. MICHAEL *comes on. He brings his automatic. He is taking the film from the camera*.

LISA (*at the window*). Stopped.

ANNA (*counts*). One. Two. Three. Four. Five. Six.

LISA. Started.

ANNA (*to* MICHAEL). Cover from the front porch. I'll do the message.

> MICHAEL *goes out.* ANNA *takes the paper from* TRENCH *and reads it. The motorbike is heard winding up the hill. As she finishes it stops outside.*

A Clear Reading of an Ultimatum

ANNA. This is why RRA have taken their action. Many of the needs of human beings can now be met. Industry and science have made a sane and contented world possible. Yet it becomes increasingly irrational. Resources are wasted and poorer countries plundered while their people starve. People are forced to seek their own ends without regard for the common good. Human relations are destroyed. Organization breaks down. Western society no longer works. As it becomes increasingly irrational so it becomes more violent. The working class cannot fit into an irrational society. Nor can it be coerced into fitting into it by education, inducement, force or fear. It is not enough to say this. We must say why. The working class becomes what it is through the very activity of its work. That is how its characteristic behaviour and opinions are formed. Clearly this cannot be changed. The alternative is as clear. Society must be changed. The working class must control not only production and distribution but also information and education. Only the working class can develop our wasting humanity and make society rational. It has created the physical structure of society. Now it must create its culture.

We cannot patiently wait for society to fall apart. Reaction armed with modern technology could make the end of this century a graveyard. That is why we have taken this action. Modern strikes create great tensions. They are a seedbed of revolution. We can therefore expect restrictions to be placed on them. This will increase conflict. Once again it will be shown that the relationships between classes are based on violence. Therefore we fight.

*

FOUR

Works Entrance.
Large notice on the wall 'No Naked Flames'.
JOHN, TERRY, RAY, BERYL. *They are very cold. One of them has a placard propped against the legs.*

RAY. Worse than bein in the bloody army. Ain this stint over? Phoo. (*He blows into his hands. Pause.*) Stood here bloody hours.
JOHN (*looks off*). Twenty past.
BERYL. Don't read Trench's clock. He'll take it off yer bleedin packet.
JOHN. And it's never bloody right.
RAY. Bugger puts it on for the start of the shift and turns it back for the end. Worked it out in the admin. Had a conference.
BERYL. Hey-up! old age P.
RAY. Don't like the look of that shopping bag.
JOHN. Here it comes.
RAY. They're making Molotov cocktails at the over-sixties.
OAP (*off*). Layabouts.

A stone is thrown onto the stage.

JOHN. Mornin granma.
OAP (*off*). Scroungers.
JOHN. Annual outin is it?

OAP (*off*). Reds. Went through the war for you lot. Day's work'd kill yer.

RAY. What's a nice old dear like you doin on the street corner? Give the flats a bad name.

JOHN. Show us yer nickers darlin. Dead borin here.

OAP (*off*). Won't laugh when they shut down.

BERYL. Why don't you shut down?

OAP (*off*). Lockin your boss up. Don't play the innocent with me. You got him.

BERYL. Go home yer silly old shit bag.

OAP (*off*). Use language.

BERYL (*throws stone back*). I said piss off.

> OAP (*off*) *screams.*

BERYL. Next time I won't miss. Piss off.

JOHN. That's right, public relations. Explain your cause politely and simply to the public. Remember your case has been misrepresented. They have a right to know. Listen before replying.

BERYL. Not my fault you ain well off. If it wasn't for us you'd be stuck in some back room with nothin to eat an no fire or light and the water froze except where it comes through the roof.

JOHN (*to himself*). Probably is.

BERYL. So go home you silly old cow. We have to fight for every tanner. Every time. Don't you call me names you silly old windbag.

OAP (*off*). Murderers!

BERYL. Bloody well will be if I catch you.

> BERYL *runs off.* OAP (*off*) *screams.*

JOHN (*to himself*). Dear-o-dear-o-lor.

OAP (*further off*). That's a threat. Goin round the law.

RAY. Chuck it in eh? Stuck here in the bloody cold. Off our rockers. The meetin'll send us back anyway.

TERRY. O yeh?

> BERYL *walks slowly back.*

RAY. The lads'll vote it won't they.

BERYL. How'm I goin t' vote?

RAY. By bloody computer.

TERRY. You chuck the strike in?

RAY. Weight of public opinion.

BERYL. Not my bloody opinion.

JOHN. Look we got a case – right?

BERYL. Right.

RAY. Did I say we ain? I come out. I'd a stayed out. I've been a paid-up member since you were in short pants Terry. This is somethin else. If they wanna play silly buggers.

BERYL. Trench is pullin a fast one. He's sunnin it out in Monte Carlo. He could pay us with what he picks up in the casino. Took all his loot back the yacht'd sink. It's time somethin changed.

RAY. I'm all for change.

JOHN. He couldn't change his address if his house burned down.

RAY. It's your common humanity.

JOHN. What the hell's that?

RAY. When you don't fight for money while some poor bleeder's fightin for his life. Keep em in the boot an throw food at em like a dog. Tie gelignite round their chest. Human bloody firework.

TERRY. Don't you learn nothin Ray?

RAY. I learn.

TERRY. Listen. We go back to work. They let Trench go?

JOHN. No. That's the nicety of it.

RAY. Now you listen Terry. What is this – Argentina?

BERYL. Not accordin to the weather forecast.

RAY. Since when we run this country with guns? What

good's guns? You got extra money you'd be robbed takin it
home. Not my sort of life mate. So? I'm all for solidarity –

BERYL. Between the ears.

RAY. Not a joke girl.

BERYL. Only a laugh.

TERRY. Look. Someone's got a gun. Who else's got a
gun?

BERYL. Annie.

RAY. Shut up.

TERRY. The law. Right – let the law fight it out.

RAY. You gotta back em up.

TERRY. Why? Who's law is it anyway? Only time a workin
man goes t' court 'e's in the dock. Anyone down your road
trainin for the bar?

BERYL. Only bar they train for s'got beer mats on it.

JOHN. An him on the floor.

RAY. O nice. Now we don't want the police. Right I'll come
down your's an turn you over.

TERRY. Look. The law's there to see it all stays where it is –
in someone else's pocket. It makes the streets safe for me to
go to work in and Trench to drive to the bank in. You can't
have one law for a millionaire and a man on the dole. It ain
on.

RAY. I'm not havin blood on my hands. Not even Trench's.
Couldn't look the wife in the face across the table.

BERYL. Wouldn't bother me.

JOHN. You wanna save Trench?

RAY. Don't tempt me.

JOHN. Then what do you want?

RAY. It's a question of standards.

JOHN. Look. (*He tries to make a diagram.*) There's the
terrorist. There's the copper. There's the worker.

RAY. Do what?

JOHN. O shit hell. (*He tries another way.*) Look. You're the
terrorist. Terry's the copper. I'm the worker. (*He walks a*

few paces away from them. Stops.) Where am I? Here? No.
(*He walks further away. Stops.*) Here? No. (*Walks as far away as he can. Stops.*) Here!

RAY. Watch that fly bastard. He'll have it off home.

JOHN. On strike. I wait quietly and say: I sweat my balls off for all the Trenchs and their rich bints, and their rich little sonnies in their posh schools, and their classy little slags of a daughter while they go round screwing multinational-millionaires an havin their pox cured in private clinics on what I put in their pockets. And I'm saying I want my money crook. I work. I've got my finger out and if the Duke of Edinburgh don't believe it he can smell it and ask that little wanker the Prince of Wales for a second opinion. That's all. Now if you lot over there are playing gunfights that's your pleasure. Bang away. I'm over here askin for what's mine.

RAY. You put a bullet in him?

JOHN. Not the point.

RAY. Answer the question.

JOHN. Yeh. Push to the top of the queue.

BERYL. We pulled it off before. Strike together, stick together. That's all it needs.

RAY. Then why nab Trench and bring the law into it?

TERRY. Well. I'm the law. (*He walks to* JOHN. *He makes no attempt to imitate a policeman's movements or the tone of his voice.*) An what are you doin sittin on the pavement in the middle of the shift? Who keeps the crooks out your pad? None of your lip. I'll give the answers. Who stops you bein run over? Who finds your kid when it's done a bunk?

JOHN. So?

TERRY. So be a good boy and picket for a few days – you look as if you could use the rest. Then back to work. You've been comin too much lately. Work. Only this time – at last – he don't. That's when I jerk him to his feet an wrap my truncheon round his stupid neck. (*He turns to* RAY *and*

BERYL.) Terrorists didn't bring the law into it. The law's
there all the time only it don't show up. Till someone
breaks the rules: the terrorists or the workers. Which is
fine. Only the rules are bent. They're not meant to find out
who wins but to keep *them* on top. They play the match but
their goal's boarded up.

RAY. Rot.

> TERRY *walks back to* BERYL *and* RAY.

TERRY. Look. (*A slight pause.*) I'm a thief. I nick Beryl's
purse. (*He does this.*)

BERYL. I know what I've got in there.

TERRY. Where's the law now? It nicks me.

RAY. Quite right.

> TERRY *throws the purse back to* BERYL.

BERYL. Next time ask.

TERRY. Now supposin I got (*He takes money from his pocket.*)
six quid in my pocket. I work for that in the factory. (*To*
JOHN:) You're Trench this time. (JOHN *comes over to him.*)
You say: I want three of them. I'm boss and that's my
profit. So Trench nicks three quid. (JOHN *takes three
notes.*) But no one shouts thief. Where's the law? So today I
don't let Trench get away with it. I take one back. But bein
law-abidin I don't nick it. I ask. And when he says no I
strike.

> TERRY *folds his arms.*

JOHN. Don't worry me sonny. I'm multinational for a start.
Doin very well out of the coolies. Mess me about and you
won't have a job to come back to. I'll give it to a computer.

TERRY. So I work it out. I say: I'd better make this strike
hurt. Fast. I picket other firms. Bring them out. Make
threats. Trench threatened me. Anyway he threatens me
all the time: his paw on my packet is a paw on my neck.
Well the moment I do that the law turns up. To get my

money back? O no – to arrest me. Why? Because I used force.

BERYL. Why didn't Trench have to use force when he took your three quid but –

BERYL.⎱
JOHN. ⎰ – you had to use it when you want some of it back?

TERRY. Because we do what we're told – like animals. He spends half of what he nicks makin sure we do. The force is always there – only he doesn't have to use it till you play it his way. Then wham! When you come down to it Trench relies on force as much as any terrorist. Only he calls his law and order. So tell me why I should pick him out of the shit when he made it himself?

BERYL. We'd be off our heads.

JOHN. Yeh! The terrorists have caught Trench at his own game!

RAY. . . . I know why. I wasn't taught much but I learned one thing. When they open up we'll get caught in the crossfire. It's us who get it in the neck.

BERYL (*bitterly*). That's right. They've got us where they want us.

JOHN (*angrily*). It's a rotten bad reason when you think of it.

Silence. They start to trudge back to the picket line.

TERRY (*stops*). How well Trench has got us trained.

RAY (*blows on his hands*). What time's Trench's clock?

JOHN. Can't you tell?

RAY. My eyes. Workin in Trench's bloody transit shed.

BERYL. Quarter to, you blind old git.

RAY (*pause. Quietly*). I hate Trench's guts more than you do. I've worked for him longer than you. When you've worked for him that long you'll find out what it's like to hate. You're in for a surprise. When I'm dead there'll still be a little man inside my head sayin: hate Trench.

TERRY. The meetin.

RAY. Take them. Don't want em nicked.

They take the placards and go.

FIVE

Boardroom.

KENDAL *and* HARRIS.

KENDAL. Just be sure what you're doing is right. These things aren't personal.

HARRIS. I'm not a fish.

KENDAL. All right! (*He calms down.*) It's all been a strain. It's good to be challenged, but . . .! (*He changes the subject.*) I can't get used to the bodyguard. No privacy. Like taking the waiter home.

HUBBARD *comes in.*

HUBBARD. Taking snaps. Came through the door like a jack-in-the-box.

KENDAL. How is he?

HUBBARD. Same as ever. Whole admin block turned up. Like a cup final. Typing pool. Messengers.

KENDAL. In his element.

HUBBARD. I want this short. And no rowing from our end. Clear?

TRENCH *comes in.*

TRENCH. I could hardly get away. What a crowd! Sorry, sorry. The typing pool gave me roses. And d'you know what the drawing office gave? An illuminated address. Imagine! I've seen another side of people today. All that smiling.

Handshakes.

HARRIS. Congratulations JT. Congratulations.

KENDAL. Well done JT. Good to see you.

HUBBARD. Looks well.

TRENCH. Thankyou. Thankyou.

HARRIS. Sit down JT.

TRENCH. Don't fuss. I've spent enough time on me bum lately. I told them you wouldn't surrender.

HARRIS. To their face? Goodlor!

TRENCH. I should congratulate *you*. Made up my mind when I came to in the boot. I said: don't whine, see it through. I got their respect. It came through in their conduct. How're your good people?

HARRIS. Upset but fine.

KENDAL. The boys were shaken up JT. You think they don't care. Then a thing like this – and they catch you by surprise. Made me feel I'd done right by them as a –

TRENCH. Fine, fine. This place – I missed it!

HARRIS. You must be tired.

TRENCH. Not a bit. It'll catch up on me tomorrow.

HUBBARD. Well you must take a long vacation somewhere that's –

TRENCH. Vacation! In the middle of a strike? Now Jimmy you surprise me. (*He wags a finger at* HARRIS *and* KENDAL.) Hope he hasn't been getting slack while I was away.

HUBBARD. Let's sit.

HUBBARD, KENDAL *and* HARRIS *sit at the boardtable.*

TRENCH. Work is what I *missed*! I want the financial statement and a full briefing on the strike. This will be good for business. O yes! Kendal I want you to –

HUBBARD. I'll run over what's been happening.

TRENCH. Of course. It's good to see you again. Mind you the security will be an erk. But it's better to be looked after by friends than enemies. I'm taking you and your wives out to dinner at –

HUBBARD. JT.

TRENCH. I'm allowed to rattle on today Jimmy without you point-of-ordering me.

KENDAL. We had a meeting while –

HUBBARD. You were away. JT we're very mindful of the services you rendered TCC.

TRENCH. Nonsense.

HUBBARD. You bore it and nurtured it till it grew. Now it wants to go out in the world.

TRENCH (*coldly*). Go public? You know my views.

HUBBARD. This moment – after the last few days – seems opportune all round. We had a meeting and decided – unanimous – that it would be right if you gave up the chairmanship.

HARRIS. We want your blessing JT.

TRENCH. You decided –. (*He stops.*)

HUBBARD. You said you wanted to fish, read your poetry books, travel. And we want to be tested. Of course you'll be hovering over us like the guardian angel. (*He hands minutes to* TRENCH.) There's the minutes JT. I think the vote of thanks will please you. No doubt –

TRENCH (*takes the minutes but doesn't look at them*). Who put this up?

HUBBARD. No inquest JT.

TRENCH. Who had this idea?

HUBBARD. We only reflected the feeling throughout the organization. We took –

TRENCH. Who had this idea?

HUBBARD. I've seen you at your best JT. Don't take the memory away.

TRENCH. What feeling in the organization? Didn't you see those people down there? My god they were crying. Little girls from central filing I didn't know.

KENDAL. JT a show of emotion means nothing.

TRENCH. They hugged me. That was the feeling down there.

HUBBARD (*trying another line*). You're not young JT. You didn't intend to go on forever.

TRENCH (*finality*). *What feeling?* You see! There was no feeling!

HUBBARD. Well the legal situation's clear. A majority of the board can make this decision. You've earned your freedom.

TRENCH. *You're* not young! That's why you – ! (*Stops. Jumps to the next idea.*) The legal situation? When I say you can't do it I don't mean it's against the law but against – (*He stops. Cannot find the words. Jumps back to the earlier idea.*) You're not young! That's why you did it! I sat and ate and slept with a gun turned on me. Those people told the truth: they said they were my enemies! But here! – What's here? (*He finds the words.*) – I say you cannot do it not because it's against the law – I know what the law is! – but because it's against common humanity! You can't! Not if you have one spark of decency! Who had this idea? (*He glances at the minutes.*) I see you gave yourself a rise.

MS LINNELL *comes in. She brings red roses.*

MS LINNELL. I hope you didn't buzz while I was down the corridor. I borrowed a silver vase from the directors' dining room. Our country dancing team won it. You remember? Mr Collins on the banjo. (*Refusing to lower her gaze.*) Roses look so fine in silver. Cut glass is vulgar unless it's very good. The girls in the outer office ask you to join them later. They've got a bottle of bubbly. Champagne.

HUBBARD. Thankyou Louise.

MS LINNELL *goes.*

TRENCH. Is she in this?

HARRIS. You might have asked after her mother. She's ill again.

HUBBARD. The rise JT. You kept us short for years. Well short.

TRENCH. *I've been sacked.* I suppose you were behind this red gang! Had me highjacked! I won't go quietly.

HARRIS. It seemed to be our duty JT.

KENDAL. You name your own handshake.

TRENCH. O I will. I will. (*To* HUBBARD.) Who takes my place?

HUBBARD. I do.

TRENCH. O I watched you. Grab, grab. I said don't judge: envy is human. Now I call my own friend: bastard! Harris, Kendal, Hubbard: you've done this. You provoked this confrontation.

HUBBARD. Only sorry to see you let yourself down.

TRENCH. God in heaven I was *kicked* down! – No. I don't say you panicked. You were under pressure. The decision was wrong. Now we'll put it right. (*He goes to the boardtable.*) As a member of the board I propose a motion: minute number seven of the twenty-ninth be struck from the record. (*He chooses a button-hole from the roses and pins it to his jacket.*) Look at these roses. (*He sits.*) I put the motion. Who will second it?

HUBBARD. You were removed from the board.

TRENCH. You hoped I would be shot. Then this scene would have been avoided. That's why you held out: to get rid of me! That's devilish! Have me shot and take flowers to the funeral! God what people are you?

HUBBARD. Your friends. We acted for the good of TCC. And you call us selfish? I'm not taking this abuse from any –

TRENCH. All right Jimmy . . . (*He walks away. For a moment he seems to be in another world.*) I wanted to come back to the world. So much. It wasn't easy. Where am I now? All my life is over. This was my life. You know that. All this while ... behind my back. I was a joke.

KENDAL. JT we're all distressed.

HUBBARD. You have no money problems. The organization's in good hands.

TRENCH. Good hands! Cut throats like you will take over the world! You stab me in the back and say it's so I don't have to shoulder the worries. You make black white! Dirt clean! Evil good! Pervert reason! My god terrorists stand things on their head. Turn values upside down. But the police go after them! You do it and vote yourself a rise! You don't rob a bank you have a cheque book! But no one hunts you, pillorizes you in the press!

HUBBARD. He's overwrought gentlemen. As far as I'm concerned you've said nothing. Let's leave it at that.

HARRIS. Here here.

TRENCH. Say I was struck dumb? That would be better? *I have a right to judge!* My god and you had obligations! O you cowards! Bastards! Behind my back! Why why why not to my face? No that wouldn't have been mean or low enough! But this – is monstrous! You act like cowards and hypocrites because that's the only way you know what you're doing!

HUBBARD. We couldn't come to you! You weren't here.

TRENCH. I was here thirty years!

HUBBARD. No one was plotting or scheming. Certainly not thirty years. Only the last few years –

HARRIS. Three.

KENDAL. Five or six at the most. Six years ago. That's when we first started to notice you'd –

TRENCH. Six years! – you schemed behind my back?

KENDAL. Plotting and scheming! No one schemed! No one spoke! It was obvious! We kept quiet till we couldn't any longer. We deserve the rise for waiting! It was obvious to

me seven years ago. At our first interview. Ten years! I've
had enough of this!

TRENCH. Five years! Ten years! A hundred years! Nothing
you say has any meaning!

HUBBARD. This meeting's closed. JT I'm sad you've taken it
like this. Though to be frank you always had to have your
own way –

TRENCH. I will not be insulted in my office!

KENDAL. It's not your office actually!

HUBBARD. Shut up Kendal. Show some sense.

TRENCH. Am I completely out or just demoted?

HUBBARD. Demoted – no. You're not the sort to –

TRENCH. Put me on the broom? Send me out on the road?
Make me the toilet man? I will not stay in a room with you.

TRENCH *goes*.

KENDAL. Could have been worse.

HUBBARD. I told you to keep quiet Kendal. What's the use
of aggravating the –

KENDAL. He shouted at me! I had to answer or he'd have had
a stroke. (*Turning nasty.*) And anyway I'm not prepared to
be spoken to like that. By him or you Hubbard. You didn't
exactly play it down.

HUBBARD. All right, all right. We've got to stick together.
You'll have to lump it.

HARRIS. Trench'll go to the press.

HUBBARD. Nine days wonder. One day the papers are full of
it. Next day some peer's set fire to his castle and run off
with the au pair. We'll say the ordeal turned his bonce. No
one ever talks sense in a crisis. You can say what you like
and it sounds normal.

HARRIS. Drink?

HUBBARD. Ta. (*He changes his mind.*) No.

HARRIS (*drinks*). Sylvia was pleased with the rise. But what's
left after tax? I ask myself is it worth it? All this fuss. I'm

beginning to be sorry you had the idea. In JT's place I
could –

HARRIS. ⎫
KENDAL. ⎬ – easily feel the same.

TRENCH *comes back.*

An Invitation

TRENCH (*quiet*). What you did was wrong. I've met many
thieves and I can tell you there's no honour among them.
No one of you will trust the others now. I shall be busy. I
have a lot to do and think about. I invited you to dinner to
celebrate my escape. Now it will be a double celebration.
I'll expect you at my house this Friday at seven. Please
cancel any other engagements you may have. I intend to go
out as if I had been working with gentlemen.

*

TRENCH *goes.*

HUBBARD (*calling after him*). That's fine JT. We put all your
private papers in sealed boxes. And the trinkets from your
desk.

HARRIS. Are we going?

KENDAL. Why not?

HUBBARD. He wants to go out playing the elder statesman.
Mean to deprive him. And he keeps an excellent table.

SIX

TRENCH's *house.*
A large painting draped in velvet.
TRENCH *comes in alone. Everyone in the scene wears formal
evening dress.*

TRENCH (*calls*). In here.

MARIAN *comes in.*

MARIAN (*sees picture*). A surprise JT?
TRENCH. Wait for the others.
MARIAN (*calls*). Quickly darlings. One of JT's surprises!

PRU *comes in.*

PRU. Gorgeous fodder JT. Always is. Don't know how you do it without a wife.
MARIAN. If you have a french cook ...

HUBBARD *enters.*

HUBBARD. Surprise?
TRENCH. Thankyou Pru.
PRU (*takes* TRENCH's *arm and leads him to one side*). I hope this little contretemps in the organization – don't worry, I won't meddle – doesn't mean there's a rift? We're pals for life aren't we JT?

KENDAL, SYLVIA *and* HARRIS *come in. They stand before the picture. Everyone except* TRENCH *carries a glass.*

KENDAL. Course you are.
PRU (*leads* TRENCH *aside*). That's right. I stay well out of anything to do with the company. But that place isn't the world thank god. Even if you boys sometimes behave as if it were. You'll have a lot more free time. I shall see even more of you. Is daddy going to be naughty and take me to a show?
TRENCH. I'm not the one who wanted a change.
PRU (*wags finger*). Naughty.
TRENCH. I'm sorry Pru. I don't respond to being patronized. Please don't. Kendal is as responsible as his colleagues for

kicking me out. Don't try and gloss it over. Did he put you
up to it?

PRU (*pout*). JT.

SYLVIA. We had a nice meal. Everyone's behaved themselves. Don't let's spoil it.

HARRIS. Really Pru you might have kept off the subject. I do
think it's rather infra to let your –

KENDAL. All Pru said was let's be friends. Damned good
advice. Even if it's sometimes difficult to take.

HUBBARD. The subject's closed.

SYLVIA. What's this surprise? (*To the girls:*) Like christmas.

TRENCH (*calmly*). Didn't your men tell you I was sacked
behind my back? While I could easily have been killed in –

HARRIS. For god's sake. (*To* PRU:) I hope you're satisfied.

MARIAN. We know JT but it's not our business. I've always
cherished our friendship and if there's –

HUBBARD. Fine. Let's leave it there.

TRENCH (*after a silence*). – a ruined hole by a gang of fanatics?
They deceived me. Under the circumstances I thought
they were deceiving their wives. As you didn't seem disturbed. Not at all. But I see you know. (*A slight bow of the
head.*) Excuse me. (*He returns to his subject.*) Still, you don't
expect *me* not to care, surely? I was sacked.

KENDAL. JT wasn't sacked. We were in a tight corner. The
strike, JT away. He couldn't be consulted. A new initiative
was necessary. Let the organization forge ahead. It was the
only way to keep our heads above water.

TRENCH. Forging ahead? Dear me. A piece of sophistry not
up to your standards. Whenever I looked at you you were
going round in circles. I say only that I don't like Pru to
talk to me as if I were in rompers or a wheel chair. Such
vulgarity should be beneath her. (*Silence. Still calm.*) And
that I don't expect to be blamed when I object to being
stabbed in the back.

HUBBARD. We're your guests. Drinking your brandy. I

suppose we listen quietly while we're torn to pieces. If that's what you want. The brandy's excellent by the way. It makes it worth it.

KENDAL. JT's wined and dined us handsomely. That's how I'll remember him. A generous colleague. Six months and we'll smile at this.

TRENCH. And so I'm not to be patronized by Pru.

PRU. O dear. Shall I put my head in the oven? I do object to being picked on. I'm not responsible for what happened.

HUBBARD. What'll you call your book JT? Must get a good title. (*To* HARRIS:) I'm not very literary but if I have to read I go for a good title.

HARRIS (*to* HUBBARD). Something from a poem.

PRU. Anything I say will mean what he wants it to. If I said sorry that would be patronizing. If I jumped out of a window I'd be doing it to make him feel guilty. (*The other women surreptitiously gesture her to be quiet.*) I will not be shushed at! (*To* TRENCH:) If you throw out all this bitterness you cut yourself off from everyone. No matter how forgiving they are.

KENDAL. Pru please.

PRU. I object to being morally blackmailed!

TRENCH. I told you I'd commissioned a painting of our team. As it then was. Now as a parting gift –

KENDAL. O JT that's really something.

TRENCH. Kendal. One advantage of being chucked out of my organization is that I don't have to put up with your innane toadying. Is that what you meant by freedom Hubbard? I've been tactful. The portrait doesn't embarrass you by commemorating me or the standards I stood for. And if I was on it you'd lose it in the basement in a week.

KENDAL. Sorry JT. You may call this toadying. But a portrait of our founder would always be –

TRENCH. Instead it reminds you of yourselves. That's important after all. If we knew what we are the world would change very fast. The little voice of truth. Most of us would have to jump off a bridge.

HUBBARD. You have to be bloody arrogant to think you always know the truth.

TRENCH (*suddenly showing his anger*). You have to be more arrogant to ignore it! You can walk by a heap of bodies and see litter. That's arrogance! Knife someone in the back because you can't look them in the face. Arrogance! Betray your friend for thirty pieces of silver and invest it on the stock exchange. All arrogance! You trip over the truth and get up and brush it off your knees. It stares at you and you smile and turn away and congratulate yourself on turning the other cheek. That's arrogance! Hypocrites wagging their heads till they drop off.

MARIAN. Am I included in that? I'd like to know.

TRENCH. Up to you. Ask Hubbard. He makes up your mind on everything.

SYLVIA. I don't see the point of these recriminations. If JT wants to –

TRENCH. What –? I'm free to speak my mind.

SYLVIA. We mustn't leave the house on its own too long Ronnie.

TRENCH. After all you live on my organization. Eat it. Educate your boys on it. Dress and sleep on it. Have fun on it. You'll be buried out of it.

HUBBARD. You screwed us for everything you could get. He stayed in the office at night pretending to work to make sure we were really working. I've come home past midnight. Marian will tell you. You lived off our fat Trench.

TRENCH (*calmly*). The picture should be unveiled by a lady.

SYLVIA (*disinterest*). So big. You must all be life size.

HUBBARD. Well let's see the –

TRENCH. Do we have a lady?

PRU. Obviously I'm out.

MARIAN. Silly Pru. I'll do it.

MARIAN gives KENDAL *her glass.*

TRENCH. I hope you have all you want – since we all seek the best we can get.

SYLVIA. Say a few words Marian. The men are messing it up.

Speech at an Unveiling

MARIAN. Well. This gesture of JT's is better than any words. What we say sounds clumsy today. We've hurt each other. I don't think we meant to. Giving and receiving – that's what shows true friendship. I believe that's what JT's trying to tell us. He's right and I've taken it to heart. We don't care for each other as we should. I know this: I'm grateful to JT. Unstintedly. We owe him. And we shouldn't forget it.

*

A smattering of polite applause: the fingers of the free hand clapped on the palm of the hand holding the glass.

SYLVIA. For he's a jolly good fellow
ALL EXCEPT TRENCH. He's a jolly good fellow
He's a jolly good fellow
And so say all of us
SYLVIA. And so say all of us

MARIAN puts her arm around JT *and kisses his cheek.*

MARIAN. God bless JT.

MARIAN and SYLVIA *drop the sheet from the picture. It is a seaside photographer's prop. It shows a tropical beach. A man flexes the biceps of one arm and holds a cigar in the hand. The other arm is round a girl. She is a blonde. Both wear bathing costume. Both have a hole on top of the neck. These are for heads to be pushed through. An ape swings in a coconut tree. A starfish is stranded on the beach. A battle cruiser is moored in the bay.*

KENDAL. Pop art.

HARRIS *starts to cry.*

HUBBARD. I call that unnecessary. Confirms the line I took.

HARRIS (*crying*). Tee-hee. Tee-hee-hee-hee. Urghaaah! (*Gropes.*) Hanky. Tee-hee. Tee-hee. Tee-hee. Er. Er. (*He doesn't stop crying till he's taken away at the end of the scene.*)

PRU. I was told I was childish.

TRENCH. Put your head in Hubbard.

HUBBARD. Tell Rogers to get our things Marian.

TRENCH. Put your head in. Show us what you are. Kendal – you? Will it show the truth? Only a game. Afraid of party games? Little Kenny can't come out and play truth he doesn't know the rules!

PRU *gives* KENDAL *her glass. She sticks her head through one of the holes in the painting.*

PRU. Howdee folks! Welcome to the lowdown! What a lovely party this is an all! (*She puts her hand through one of the holes and makes an obscene gesture.*) We're havin one hell of a ball! This here is the greatest strip show on earth! The Trench festival of striperama! Come and have a peep folks! (*She starts throwing her clothes over the top of the picture.*) We're really getting down to the bare facts.

HUBBARD. Get out of the way Trench.

TRENCH. Circus acts! You smashed me! One man? There're plenty more! You had duties and obligations. You betrayed all that. Not some little milkman who cheats on his takings. A few quid a week and he can't sleep at night in

case he's sacked. A child who steals a few coppers and
spends its days in terror. You cheat from the top! And
sleep well on it! Even when you do good you smash! You're
a plague!

PRU. It's strip-strip-stripping time!

KENDAL (*Bored*). Pru shut up.

PRU (*sticks a leg from the side of the canvas*). What the hell they
wanna put them holes on different levels for? How's a gal
supposed to get her tits through? I'm gonna complain to
the manager! They wanna hire a freak!

> SYLVIA *tries to get* PRU *to dress. She chases her round the
> room, holding out her clothes. She tries to drape her in the
> sheet.* KENDAL *sits on the empty floor and sips his drink. He
> has the empty glasses of the three women.*

SYLVIA. Stop it. Pru. Stop it. This is terrible. Look how
Ronnie's upset. (*She goes to* KENDAL.) Mr Kendal stop
your wife.

> SYLVIA *chases* PRU *round the room.* MARIAN *wanders
> round the others smiling reassuringly and making calming
> gestures.* HARRIS *cries.*

PRU. I charge extra for streaking! You wanna stop a strike!
Just let me run round the factory and those men'll follow
me right in through the main gate.

KENDAL (*calmly*). O my god.

MARIAN. Whatever the other's did you have no right to treat
me and Sylvia like this.

HARRIS. Tee-hee. Tee-hee. Hee-hee-hee. Not fair. O tee-
hee-hee. Urgh! Urgh! No right to treat me like this. I told
them what it would be. They brushed me aside. Tee-hee.
Tee-hee. Tee-hee.

SYLVIA (*thumps* HARRIS' *back*). For god's sake Ronnie stop
it. You're showing all your teeth. You look ridiculous.

KENDAL (*Bored*). Pru stop it.

SYLVIA *sits on the ground and has hysterics. She throws her shoes at the wall. She drums her heels on the floor. She beats the ground with her fists. She screams.* HUBBARD *throws his cigar on the floor and jumps on it.* MARIAN *wanders round smiling.* PRU *is naked.*

PRU. Let the light in! Hey big spender!

TRENCH. O god o god o god! That there's no justice! People like you – smash smash smash! You smile and read reports and smash!

MARIAN. Let my husband pass!

TRENCH. O are you late for an appointment? Buying up poison? Cornering the market in bones? Paying your hit man? Fixing some little clerk with figures to sell? A secretary in industrial espionage? Selling your family grave for redevelopment?

HARRIS. Tee-hee. Tee-hee. Tee-hee.

SYLVIA. For god's sake cover your face with your hanky.

TRENCH *herds* HUBBARD, MARIAN, SYLVIA *and* HARRIS *out. He goes out with them.*

TRENCH (*as he goes*). Out! (*Off.*) Go and get on with your business! Show us what you are! Then we're warned!

SYLVIA (*off, screams*).

KENDAL. O my god. Showing your tits to JT.

PRU. I'm not having that old bore preach at me. It's the last time I chat up anyone for you.

KENDAL *is collecting her clothes and handing them to her. She dresses.*

PRU. I feel high. Would you take me to a night club?

KENDAL. Great.

PRU. You'll be managing director soon. There's not much left in Hubbard's cupboard. I shall enjoy your new position. And I'm putting in for a rise. Tonight sweetie.

TRENCH *comes back.*

TRENCH. If you'd like the silver knock the butler on the head. The keys to my safe are in the desk. You'll find some small coins in my overcoat pocket on your way out. If you unscrew the light bulbs be careful.

KENDAL. 'Pacific 203' or 'Silver Orchid'?

PRU. Both.

PRU *and* KENDAL *go. She carries the last of the clothes with her.*

TRENCH. Rid of them.

HARRIS *comes back through another door.*

HARRIS. Tee-hee. O dear look what you've done. No cause to speak to me like that JT. JT tee-hee. Tee-hee. Not spoken to like that since I was a child. Tee-hee. I'm your friend. I knew it was wrong.

SYLVIA *comes on with a handful of tissues.*

SYLVIA. Ronald.

HARRIS. So harsh. So harsh.

SYLVIA. O god you're dribbling. Wipe your chin on these tissues.

HARRIS. Tee-hee.

SYLVIA *and* HARRIS *go.* TRENCH *sits alone on the floor.*

TRENCH. I'm afraid.

Part Two

ONE

Derelict House.
The photographer's prop is in the middle of the room.
Empty. LISA *comes in. She wears everyday clothes. She stares at
the picture. She looks round. She goes to the window. She gestures
to someone outside.* TRENCH *comes in through the side door. He is
dirty and unshaven. His clothes are of good quality but dirty. He
eats a biscuit.*

TRENCH. You're trespassing.
LISA. O.
TRENCH. Heard the car.
LISA. Sorry.
TRENCH. What d'you want?
LISA. Just passing.
TRENCH. No, you stopped.
LISA. Saw this.
TRENCH. Stop at everything you see?
LISA. Looked deserted. I want a place to do up.
TRENCH. Not for sale.
LISA (*picture*). What's that?
TRENCH. Mine.
LISA. O. (*Starts to go.*) Sorry I bashed in. (*Stops.*) You live
   here?
TRENCH. Yes.
LISA. On your own?
TRENCH. My business.
LISA. Why d'you live here?
TRENCH. I bought it.
LISA. Yes. (*She turns to go.*)

TRENCH. Sat by a window for a long time. Then sold up and came here. Was a prisoner here once.

LISA. There are no shops.

TRENCH. Bike to the village.

> MICHAEL *comes in. He stands in the doorway behind* LISA.

TRENCH (*points at* MICHAEL). Look.

LISA. My friend.

MICHAEL (*to* LISA). All right?

LISA. Yes. He lives here.

TRENCH. Rut rut rut.

MICHAEL (*picture*). What's that?

TRENCH. Mine. You can have a drink.

MICHAEL. Don't bother.

> TRENCH *goes out.* MICHAEL *moves so that he can watch him.*

LISA. He doesn't recognize us.

MICHAEL. What's he doing here?

LISA. He *lives* here. Off his head.

MICHAEL. Must be. Let's go.

LISA. No. I'm enjoying it. It's quite safe.

> MICHAEL *stands by the door to watch* TRENCH.

LISA. What's he doing?

MICHAEL. Head in the cupboard. (*He glances round the room.*) Spooky. (*Picture.*) And what the hell's that?

LISA (*looks through the window*). I thought I'd never forget it. I'd even forgot the colour of the walls. (*She puts her hand on the window pane.*) We weren't strong.

MICHAEL. Strong enough.

LISA. No. We should have shot it out.

MICHAEL. Waste. We'd been grassed. If the pigs knew this place they must have known our get-out.

LISA. We could have forced a plane out of them and –

MICHAEL. No. We had to go into hiding on our own. Who'd have given us asylum? Once the pigs were tipped off we didn't stand a chance.

LISA. We should have shot it out. We weren't here to save our necks.

MICHAEL. Don't play the hero. It'll be different next time. Factories strike – you can rely on that.

LISA. What if we still have the grass?

MICHAEL. We weeded. What else can we do?

LISA. I don't trust anyone.

MICHAEL. Not me?

LISA. Nope. If you trust someone it's betraying the rest. (*Staring through the window.*) The heather. I bolted through it and called myself a traitor.

> MICHAEL *gives a warning sound to* LISA.
> TRENCH *comes back with a can of beer.*

TRENCH. You'll have to share.

LISA (*takes the can*). Thanks. (*She drinks.*) Good.

TRENCH (*calmly*). It's strange not meeting people. But then, I'm no longer soiled by them . . . Their horizon is the end of a pig trough. They tear the clothes from the living and the rags from the dead. Till they die and go in a plastic coffin to be burned. They have violence on their faces as if they'd been painted by a savage. Their hands are frayed ends of rope taken from old parcels. Voices like sounds coming out of a wound. I turned away while they spoke. Costs too much to be polite . . . (*He half notices they haven't understood. He tries again.*) Every year the ants came to my garden. A long line going under the fence. A few dragged parts of an insect. There's nothing else. So I left.

> LISA *has given* MICHAEL *the can. He holds it without drinking. He passes it back to* LISA.

MICHAEL. Finish it.

> LISA *drinks*.

MICHAEL. Let's go.
LISA. Thanks.
TRENCH. Pleasure.
LISA. Bye.

> LISA *and* MICHAEL *go*.

TWO

Derelict House.
Night. Noises off. TRENCH *flat against the wall.*
The door opens. Torches. LISA *runs in. She puts down a bundle.*
She catches TRENCH *in her torch.*

LISA. Stay there. Blow your head off.

> ANNA *comes in.* LISA *keeps the torchlight on* TRENCH.

ANNA (*puts blankets on the floor*). Jesus.
LISA. Bloody light?
ANNA. Cover the windows.
LISA. Bloody light. Bloody light. (*Searching.*) I thought it
was here.

> ANNA *covers the window.* LISA *finds the light and switches*
> *it on.*

> MICHAEL *comes in with a bundle. The terrorists carry guns.*
> *They wear balaclavas.*

ANNA. Get the car away!

> ANNA *goes off.*

MICHAEL. Tins.
ANNA (*Off*). Get rid of the car! Everything out?
MICHAEL. All you need. I checked.
ANNA (*Off*). And the boot?
MICHAEL. I checked.

ANNA *returns.*

ANNA. Hop it!
MICHAEL (*to* LISA). Manage?
ANNA (*moving the photographer's prop to the wall*). Of course.
MICHAEL. Tomorrow.
ANNA. Early! Very early!
MICHAEL. If I can. You may have to be patient.
ANNA. No! Early! Otherwise we've had it!
MICHAEL (*to* LISA *as she stacks things*). I'll give you a hand.
ANNA. No! Go! We can manage!

MICHAEL *is on his knees. He reaches for her. He presses his face into her.* ANNA *sorts things. Then she goes out.*

ANNA (*off*). I'll do first watch.

LISA *gets* MICHAEL *to his feet. They go after* ANNA. TRENCH *stays against the wall.* LISA *and* ANNA *return.* THEY *carry a figure in a white boiler suit, no shoes, white socks and a white hood. The face isn't seen. The legs and hands are tied. It looks like a giant maggot. They lay it on the floor.*

ANNA (*peering through the window*). Move those. All over the place.

Off, the sound of a car starting and driving away. LISA *stacks things.*

LISA. Still got a grass.

ANNA (*to* TRENCH). Do what you're told. You'll be all right. We'll go in the morning.

LISA. Don't like running.

ANNA. No one does. They'll get us a place tomorrow.

LISA. If that's not tipped off. Who is it?

The WHITE FIGURE *pounds its heels on the ground.*

LISA. O god bog time already! (*To* ANNA.) Have I got to be bloody nurse maid again? (*To* WHITE FIGURE.) Get up. Up. D'you want to go or don't you?

LISA *gets the* WHITE FIGURE *to its feet and drags it out.*

TRENCH. I know you. You were here before.

ANNA. Who comes here?

TRENCH. No one.

ANNA. You'd better tell me. You'll get your head shot off if someone comes.

TRENCH. No one.

ANNA (*turning back to the window*). They will after today's fun.

TRENCH. Will you take me with you?

ANNA. I'll see. We were on the way to a hideout. It was crawling with police. We'd been grassed. You can put us up for one night. Do what you're told you'll be all right.

TRENCH. Stay here.

ANNA. Here? They'll come.

TRENCH. I told you –

ANNA. They'll check tomorrow. Another strike at TCC.

TRENCH. O . . . that's Hubbard?

ANNA (*shakes her head*). It went wrong.

TRENCH. Wait in the hills. Come down when they've gone.

ANNA. No. Need somewhere safe. Can't trust you. Can't trust ourselves.

TRENCH. The informer. Always one of your own . . . You left

me tied up like a pig at the butcher's cart. Police cut me
free. I went home. My friends killed me. (*His voice has
sunk. He's almost talking to himself. He raises his voice.*
Could be anyone. That girl. You. Perhaps that man's
driven off to the police. Writing your names down now.

LISA *comes back dragging the* WHITE FIGURE. *It falls.*

LISA. Not here! Get up! Over there! Got the runs. Shit
scared. I said *down*!

The WHITE FIGURE *lies on the floor.*

LISA. Cock up.
ANNA. We're still in control.

The WHITE FIGURE *pounds its heels on the ground.*

LISA. O god wait. I'm not trotting in and out with you the
whole bloody night. Bloody wait.
ANNA. Put that torch out.

LISA *switches off a torch.*

ANNA. D'you want to eat?
LISA. Couldn't keep it down.
ANNA. We take it in turns to sleep. Keep calm and rest.
LISA. I know! – What's the point of holding onto him?
Should have dumped him. What's he worth? Get more
back on a nonreturnable bottle.
ANNA. A hostage is a hostage. (*Slight pause.*) It'll stink the
place out.

LISA *gets the* WHITE FIGURE *to its feet.*

LISA. Up! Drop him on the motorway and clear off.
ANNA. No car.
LISA. In the morning.
ANNA. H.Q. decides.
LISA (*taking the* WHITE FIGURE *out*). Shut up with a loony
and a human liability with the runs.

LISA *and the* WHITE FIGURE *go.*

TRENCH. It's safe in the hills.
ANNA (*looks at her watch*). News. (*Radio.*)

THREE

Boardroom.
HUBBARD, KENDAL, HARRIS, LORD BIGDYKE, POLICE
CHIEF. KENDAL'S *forehead is plastered.*

BIGDYKE. They hope to weaken you by creating a feeling of
fatalism. We won the first round. Now they show us it was
a pyrrhic victory. The problem comes back unsolved. It
always will. They'll go on harassing your organization
till your spirit breaks and you collapse – or we break
them.
HARRIS. They could have got me this time. Any of us. We
have a right to protection. We pay our taxes. I can't run an
organization in these conditions.
POLICE CHIEF (*smiles*). You could resign.
HUBBARD. Look. You sorted it out last time. What are you
doing now.
POLICE CHIEF. Can't discuss it with you. Can *tell* you
something. In private. (*Smiles.*) A nasty setback. We had
certain information –
KENDAL. You've got a plant?
POLICE CHIEF. We surrounded a certain location. Getting
clever. They didn't turn up. They sent a scout. (*Smiles.*)
Now we don't know where the hell they are.
HARRIS. A never-ending oneway street!
POLICE CHIEF. On the asset side the pressure's off. They
didn't get Mr Kendal.

BIGDYKE. Though we treat all victims the same.

POLICE CHIEF. Yes – but the pressure's off. What can they do? Sheepishly send him back. We should all be feeling very pleased.

BIGDYKE. Let's hope. But it ought never to have happened. From now on whenever there's industrial unrest at TCC precautions must be even more stringent. I hope that is now understood. (*To* POLICE CHIEF.) I thought you were responsible for their safety?

POLICE CHIEF (*smiles*). And your's Lord Bigdyke.

BIGDYKE (*turns away*). This could attract imitators. Terrorism could become as common as street accidents. If it did the country would be turned into a police state. All the advantages our fathers worked for – our science and technology – could be perverted to evil ends.

POLICE CHIEF. Don't worry Lord Bigdyke we don't seek that sort of power. (*To the others:*) But we're ready. O the nature of the beast has changed. Once the ordinary man policed himself. The sight of the uniform was enough. With the odd tap from the truncheon and the occasional hanging. Church and school did their job then. Not now. Press doesn't help: muck. Still, technology's on our side – if that's what you meant Lord Bigdyke? We don't seek it but we're ready.

BIGDYKE. The strike negotiations go on in the usual way. This is an industrial matter not a political one. Terrorism must be seen to be a crime. If ever the public saw it as politics we'd be lost. (*He stands.*) We sit tight till we hear from them. Goodday.

HUBBARD. ⎫
HARRIS. ⎬ Goodbye.

KENDAL. Thankyou Lord Bigdyke. Goodbye.

LORD BIGDYKE *goes.*

POLICE CHIEF. How d'you feel?

HUBBARD. Shit scared.

POLICE CHIEF (*pleasantly*). Glad to hear it. A proper assessment of the situation. Bye bye.

POLICE CHIEF *goes*.

HARRIS. You know what worries me.

HUBBARD. Don't tell me.

HARRIS. There's no way out. If I left the country, burned my papers, my home, my clothes, changed my sex and divorced the wife, put the dog to sleep, had plastic surgery and closed my bank account I still wouldn't be safe. These louts have diseased imaginations –

HUBBARD. A diseased lack of it.

HARRIS. – In their eyes I'll always be guilty. They'll track me down anywhere.

HUBBARD. No one's changing their sex. We stick together.

MS LINNELL *comes in*.

MS LINNELL. Messers Gate and Lamb.

HUBBARD (*calls*). Come in.

TERRY *and* GATE *come in*.

HUBBARD. What a day.

GATE (*noncommittally*). What a day.

HUBBARD. Take a seat.

GATE, KENDAL *and* HARRIS *sit*. MS LINNELL *shows* TERRY *to his chair. She takes shorthand notes*.

HUBBARD. You know the situation. Your claim for twenty per cent has been on the table three weeks. On Monday you took the men out. Yesterday Mr Kendal's car was rammed. Mr Kendal had the foresight to swap hats with his chauffeur.

KENDAL. In this day and age you can't even wear your own hat.

HUBBARD. In the cuffuffle they took the chauffeur in mistake.

TERRY (to GATE). What's the chauffeurs' union say about that?

KENDAL. He wasn't in a union.

TERRY (*To* KENDAL). Makes our point.

A Negotiations Speech

HUBBARD. Four things. First. For the second time an industrial dispute at TCC has resulted in the taking of a hostage. You know what the country thinks.

TERRY. I don't. I know what the papers think.

HUBBARD. They say by staying out you support the terrorists.

KENDAL. Only possible conclusion.

GATE. No. They've got nothing to do with us.

HARRIS. Public opinion! Striking for terrorism!

KENDAL. They've put you on the spot Mr Gate. What comes first: a few quid in your pocket or the security of your families?

GATE. If you're that bothered why don't you give in?

HUBBARD. My god I would to get that man off. But as you'll see that would be doing all of us a disservice.

GATE. How?

HUBBARD. We'll come to it. Secondly. When Mr Trench was taken the hostage was what you'd call a class enemy. A boss. Someone like me – who regrets the passing of rickets. Even a cat that didn't know it had whiskers could tell how you'd react to that. This is different. The chauffeur earns less than you –

TERRY. Shouldn't work for him.

HUBBARD. An elderly man who never harmed anyone. Noted for his kindness. Mr Kendal tells me he didn't like to blow the horn even at lady drivers. Only last summer he rescued a little boy from the boating pond. Shows his medals in a glass case. Old Mr Kendal passed him on to young Mr Kendal with a glowing reference. The wife's poorly. There's a daughter. She came late to bless his grey hairs. And a dog. I'm not trying to get your sympathy for them. They already have it. But this time it's not an exploiter. It's one of your own.

TERRY. Because he pinched his bloody hat.

KENDAL. I don't like your tone. It was his idea. I thought as soon as they got a close look they'd let him go. A routine precaution. I'm not to blame if your pals can't see the difference between an old man and a –

GATE. Our pals?

HUBBARD. Let's say supporters.

HARRIS. My god why don't you condemn them? Bawl them out! Last time not one word! Whatever your grouses you can't say your standard of living justifies that! Four thousand Pontius Pilates washing their hands in their automatic washing machines and drying them in their spin dryers. Mr Trench brutally shot down – well it's only by the grace of god he wasn't! – and it's nothing to do with you? Will you speak up against this outrage?

TERRY (*Quietly*). No. Every penny we get we fight for. You think words come cheap –

GATE. Terry.

TERRY. Yes sir no sir. Well they're not cheap anymore. (*He taps the demand.*) That's the price.

HUBBARD. Please please please. Let's keep to the point.

TERRY. If he talks to me like that I'm leaving.

HUBBARD. Thirdly. We've got to show these fanatics their tactics don't wash. No organization can work under these threats. Can't you see?

GATE. Mr Hubbard the men are asking for a fair return –

HUBBARD. Hold on. Haven't finished. Look. This is an argument to reason – not emotion. Suppose we cave in.

Who did we cave in to? You? Tell that to the terrorists. They'll say they did it. Isn't that right? And it won't end there. These vermin – others are watching from their holes. If they get away with it the rest will move in. You've proved it works –

TERRY. You're enjoying this Hubbard. It's not negotiation it's blackmail.

HUBBARD. Next time a bomb goes off in a shopping precinct and some child loses its eyes or legs or some girl buying her trousseau gets killed – it's happened! – that's part your doing –

TERRY (*stands*). I'm off.

> GATE *motions him to stay.* TERRY *stops halfway to the door.*

HUBBARD. Part your doing. Can you deny it? You insist on the full claim – and you're taking money with blood on it. You're not evil men. You didn't make the situation anymore than I did. But the consequences of the situation can't be avoided. You want power? If you have power you have to accept responsibility. Well responsibility means you don't keep saying mine mine mine. You forgo your interest and consider the rest. So last point. They've put you in a position you have to show them where you stand. The only decent thing you can do is take *less* than we offered. The rest is blood money.

*

TERRY (*to* GATE). Come on Joe.

GATE. Mr Hubbard you're not just bosses here. Your class is boss out there. Terror's your responsibility. Don't hang it round our neck.

KENDAL. If Trench had come home in a box at least he could buy the best funeral. What'll you say to the driver's widow?

HUBBARD. Gentlemen. All our hands are tied. What is there

left? Our common humanity. Our decency. I want that man back safe and sound. If you settle for less – as in all conscience I think you must – they can't kill him.

The POLICE CHIEF *comes in.*

POLICE CHIEF (*looks at* TERRY *and* GATE). These ...?
HUBBARD. Union.
POLICE CHIEF. Come outside.

The POLICE CHIEF, KENDAL, HUBBARD, HARRIS *and* MS LINNELL *go out.*

TERRY. What's all that about?
GATE. Must have found him.
TERRY. Was he serious about the cut?
GATE. They try anything.

> GATE *stands by the door in a posture of intense listening. He strains to hear what's happening outside.* TERRY *stares at the board table.*

A Public Soliloquy

TERRY. How often do we use a table like that? When we're married? They lay us on something smaller when we're dead. They use it every day. (*He sits in* HUBBARD'*s chair.* GATE *stays at the door in the posture of intense listening.*) If we were here the brotherhood of man would not come overnight. But it would be harder for inhumanity to prosper. Why? Because in everything we did we'd seek only for the welfare of mankind. No-one who's sat in these chairs till now can say that. All their trading was based on competition, aggression and inequality. Under the pressure of daily life these things turn into conflict, violence and injustice. All that comes from their hands. It's more surprising that their world's stayed together for so long than that it now falls apart. One half the effort and struggle needed to hold it together would make a new world. It's far easier to make things better than to keep them as they are. Nor is the cost so great. The world that can't change loses all that it has.

*

MS LINNELL *and* HARRIS *come in.* MS LINNELL *brings a silver tea pot, tea cup and saucer, silver tea spoon, silver milk jug and silver sugar bowl on a silver tea tray.*

MS LINNELL. The typing pool's in tears. (*Looking straight in* TERRY'*s face and giving him the tea things.*) Mr Hubbard, your tea.

MS LINNELL *goes.*

GATE. What's happening?

TERRY *pours tea, adds milk, stirs it and drinks.* HARRIS *sits.*

HARRIS (*calm*). The government will take it out of our hands now. Have I got to be torn apart for the sake of one little chauffeur? Especially Kendal's! I'm out of my depth. You men will ruin everything. (*On the verge of tears.*) It's all right. I'm perfectly in control. (*Outburst.*) Action! Action! Action against anarchy and sabotage! Action!

HUBBARD, KENDAL, POLICE CHIEF *and* MS LINNELL *come in.* MS LINNELL *brings her pad and pencil.*

GATE. What's happening?

HUBBARD. The people holding Mr Kendal's chauffeur have put a price on his head. TCC to pay. One hundred thousand pounds or he's shot in three days. One hundred thousand pounds for a chauffeur.

HARRIS (*outburst*). Ludicrous! Ludicrous! The whole world's laughing at us.

MS LINNELL. You've drunk Mr Hubbard's tea!

TERRY. You gave it to me.

GATE. I must get back to the office. Excuse me. Terry.

    GATE *goes.*

KENDAL. On top of the twenty per cent?

POLICE CHIEF. I forgot to ask.

KENDAL. Lord Bigdyke will be finding out.

POLICE CHIEF. I should think he's looking up a suitable quotation. He once quoted Latin at an anarchists' punch-up.

TERRY (*still in* HUBBARD's *chair*). Beautiful.

HUBBARD. He's unwell. Get a nurse.

MS LINNELL. Shock. I've worked in first aid. Glass of water. No not on the top of the tea. Keep them warm. (*She takes off her woolly and holds it out to him.*)

TERRY. Beautiful.

HUBBARD. What's beautiful?

TERRY. Common humanity? Decency? Brotherhood? Well what's he worth? How much? How much? (*A moment's silence. He gives an inarticulate shout. He sits on the back of the chair with his feet on the seat.*) Will you pay?

KENDAL. A hundred thousand pounds?

MS LINNELL (*holding out the woolly*). Get off that chair. It's walnut.

TERRY. Will you pay?

KENDAL.   ⎫
        ⎬ Of course not!
HARRIS.   ⎭

TERRY (*violently*). Then where's your common humanity? O more than that's paid for some of them! *They* get off! They've got money in the bank! (*He shouts again.*) Haa! How much? How much? What's he worth?

    LORD BIGDYKE *comes in.*

(*Threateningly.*). Hubbard you lectured me! Common humanity? Brothers? So how much? *Nothing!* O you liars! You've got to admire the beauty of the situation.

HUBBARD. The meeting's over. So is the office party. We'll be in touch. Lord Bigdyke please sit down.

MS LINNELL *follows* TERRY *holding out her woolly.*

MS LINNELL. You must be kept warm.
TERRY. Lord Bigdyke is it?
BIGDYKE. How d'you do?
TERRY. I'll tell you when there'll be common humanity: when the driver's worth as much as the passenger.

TERRY *goes.*

BIGDYKE. Abiit excessit evasit erupit.
POLICE CHIEF. You see what the force has to contend with in the general public.
HARRIS. I know Kendal likes to play Napoleon. But he's not. Nowhere near. We're all out of our depth. (*To* BIGDYKE:) And you!
BIGDYKE. They do keep one step ahead.
HARRIS (*to* POLICE CHIEF): You must take over.
BIGDYKE. The government has made a law against terrorism and it will do its best to enforce it. But whether you give the money is a moral dilemma. Morality is the responsibility of the individual. The government is not the keeper of your conscience. That would make it totalitarian. In the end the fate of a nation is decided not by its rulers but by those who are ruled. (*Quiet despair.*) I would not hide from you my belief that the times are dark. The Tiber cannot be defended by noble minds and beautiful phrases.
HARRIS. I resign. I'm off to Australia. My brother-in-law has a sheep-farm. I shall lead sheep. Men don't want to be led anymore. They prefer chaos.

HARRIS *goes.*

KENDAL (*pose*). Lord Bigdyke TCC stands firm. That's still

the tradition of our company. Whoever's taken: me or – as it happens – the driver.

HUBBARD. You forget the sales. All very well Kendal making gestures. Fine if you're in the priesthood or the civil service. (*Smiling.*) I'm sorry, we're business men. We must behave like business men – and carry out our obligation to the business and our workers. If we say no and they dump his corpse on our doorstep sales could drop to nothing. If we fork out they might rise. The mighty giant helping the little man. I know which I'd choose. I know which the chauffeur would choose. And I know what's best for the country. I'm surprised at you jumping in with both feet Kendal.

> HARRIS *comes back with* MS LINNELL. *He's trying to button himself into his overcoat.* MS LINNELL *helps. As he listens to* HUBBARD *he starts to unbutton it.*

HARRIS. I'm prepared to work out a month. On condition I get a bullet proof suit, an armoured car and a –

KENDAL. You can't run a company like that.

HUBBARD. That's the only way you can run a company.

KENDAL. But you don't know sales will rise. (*Grudgingly.*) Probably yes. (*Interested.*) But how much?

HUBBARD. Get a market survey. That's the best bible. With the right publicity. Something beautiful: a bird flying out of a cage. What's a hundred thousand pounds to the future of the company? Just when we're going public. Couldn't have chosen better timing ourselves. Price could have been better. Looks a bit mean. I'd have preferred two hundred thou'. But they've got us by the short and curlies there. We can't fix the figure.

HARRIS (*hands his overcoat to* MS LINNELL). Jimmy's right. A ceremony. Informal – but a large hall. Chauffeur's wife with her arms round Hubbard. Man and wife reunited.

Have you seen the daughter's boobs? Can't remember
what your chauffeur looks like.

FOUR

Outside TERRY's *House.*
JOHN *alone.* TERRY *rides on a scooter. He stops and switches off
the engine.*

JOHN. Well?
TERRY. Yeh. Misses when you rev.
JOHN. Nothin. Plugs. (*He works on the machine.*) Never let
me down.

> TERRY *goes into the house.* RAY *and* BERYL *come on.*

JOHN (*working*). Lo.
RAY AND BERYL. Lo.
RAY. Terry anywhere?
JOHN. Indoors.
RAY. Still floggin that pile of scrap?
JOHN. Yeh. Gotta get the money.
BERYL. Ray wants to go back.
JOHN. That what you come round for?
BERYL. Yeh.
RAY. You with us?
JOHN. He's gonna buy the bike. If we agree the figure.
RAY. He's thick but he's not that thick.

> TERRY *comes out of the house. He brings two small bottles
> of pop.*

TERRY. O. Want a drink?
BERYL. No thanks.
TERRY (*hands* JOHN *a bottle*). Fix it?
JOHN (*working*). They wanna go back.

TERRY. O yeh.

RAY. You with us?

TERRY. No.

RAY. It's one of our own.

TERRY. Ray they won't kill him.

BERYL. You can't say that Terry.

TERRY. Look. It's a stunt. For publicity. They'll make their
point and let him go. Listen.

A Workman's Biography

Hundred thousand pounds? Waitin in drafty corners. Sittin outside nightclubs till three in the morning. Ain done
his health no good. Say ninety thousand. Gettin on.
Eyesight's goin. Bad hearin. Has to ask 'where to' twice.
Say eighty thousand. Wife not too good. Needs nursin.
Can't manage the late nights. Seventy thousand. Mrs
Kendal wants somethin younger so she can score off the
other rich slags. And she'd like to pull into a lay-by on the
way home. Which is bad when you're gettin on. Fifty
thousand. Votes Tory to please the boss. Thirty thousand.
Lives in two pokey rooms cause the rent's controlled. No
central heatin. Stairs bad for his heart. Twenty thousand.
Reads The Sun. Ten thousand. Never double crossed a
customer. Never put one over on the public. Five
thousand. Nerves goin. Kendal bawls him out in the hold
ups for not drivin out on top of the other traffic. One
thousand. On tablets to get himself started in the mornins.
Very dodgy. Bloody hell – we owe you!

*

BERYL. You don't know that Ray.

TERRY. What else could it be? Publicity like that's worth
more than a hundred thousand! They'll make their point
an let him go.

RAY. Great – if they were right in the head. They don't work
    things out like you an me. They're nutters! I'm goin back.
    I'd go back if they had you or your kid. You wouldn't for
    us!

TERRY. If the meetin says no?

RAY. Yeh: back.

JOHN. Okay now. Try it.

TERRY. Not happy if it misses.

JOHN. I fixed it! Try it on the block.

TERRY. Haven't got time.

JOHN. Bloody hell. What I bin fixin it for? *I'll* bloody try it on
    the block.

   JOHN *starts the motor and drives out.*

TERRY. All right they're nutters. You go back. TCC won't
    pay that sort of money. So he's killed anyway.

RAY. I don't know about all that. I'm havin nothin t'do with
    any of it. That's where I stand.

A Speech

TERRY. You don't! Look. They got the money: let *them* give!
    Yes sir no sir was good enough for our fathers. Well it's not
    good enough anymore. What good did it do them? We
    always climb down at the crunch. Where will that get us?
    Are we suddenly so powerful we can change the world by
    bein kind? It's been tried. It didn't work. (*Almost hits*
    RAY.) You *don't* know where you stand! (*Quietens down.*)
    You fought the war. Did you jack it in when they started
    bombin back home? They were your own. No. You went
    on. It's the same now. You're in a fight. So stand there!
    That's the only way to give anythin any value anymore.
    You do anythin else and it's wasted. Kindness? Humanity?
    Decency? They destroyed all that! (RAY *doesn't answer.*)
    What does it say on this bottle? (*Pop bottle.*) Use contents

and dispose of. They put that on all of us! We're worthless! Use and destroy! They'll take your bit of kindness and suck it down into their swamp! We say no – or we're finished!

*

RAY. An if he gets shot?
TERRY. He's shot.

Immediately the sound of the scooter. John rides in on it.

RAY. Jesuschriss. I never thought I'd hear a mate of mine say that. I want to puke.
BERYL. It's no use sayin that Ray.
TERRY (*to* JOHN): What about you?
JOHN. Not decided. Look I'll knock ten quid off for a quick sale.

TERRY picks up the two empty bottles and goes.

JOHN. Thanks! What you wanna upset him for?
BERYL. There are other things apart from your pocket.
JOHN. I can't help it if I need the money. Me maintenance arrears. You try tellin that to the magistrate. You could've waited.

JOHN drives off on the scooter.

BERYL. You said you wouldn't shout.

RAY and BERYL go.

FIVE

Derelict House.
ANNA, LISA, WHITE FIGURE.
LISA *sits on guard at the window. She is draped in a blanket.*
ANNA *lies in a sleeping bag.*

ANNA. Sleep?

LISA. Hm.

ANNA. Good.

LISA (*pours herself coffee from a flask*). Coffee?

ANNA. No thanks.

LISA. Did you?

ANNA. No. Too peaceful to sleep. The night went so quickly.
I've been going over it and asking if we're right. If not I'd
give myself up. There's no alternative. It's done. Now we
let it take its course.

LISA. Perhaps the grass has done it again.

ANNA. Only Michael knows we're here.

LISA. I can't kill him.

A Poem

ANNA. Last time it was winter. The stream had frozen slowly
into strange shapes. I walked up it over the hills. There was
a heron wandering about in the sky. A heron is a bird. It
flies. But it was lost. When the water froze it had nothing to
eat.

LISA. And?

ANNA. It has to come down to live. I have visions – but to
change the world you come down. Not because we want to.
You only change things on the terms in which they're able
to change. Not by the visions. The struggle in the dirt. I
don't want to kill him. The world's mad. We're trapped in
it. I'd do anything to change it. I'd kill him.

*

TRENCH *has wandered in. He's draped in a blanket.*

TRENCH. Nice. You sit there with your guns and watch your
corpse. Arguing about death. It'll come to nothing. The
world's already ended except for the crying. One day
someone in an office made a decision – probably minor –

and history took a fatal turn. We were condemned. We didn't notice. The day passed and we went on. By the evening it was all over. This generation won't see the century out.

ANNA. You still belong to your business friends.

TRENCH (*calmly*). Not true.

ANNA. You saw through them but you put nothing in their place. They're a civilization without morals. You're a culture of despair. Absurd and empty. You let them think they can still produce a human soul. A hermit to sit on an island and tell them they're nothing. They admire you. You give them the illusion they have a moral sense.

TRENCH (*calmly*). Not true, not true.

LISA. He can't listen anymore.

ANNA. D'you hate us?

TRENCH. No, I see things as they are.

> *As* TRENCH *talks* ANNA *unpacks a quarter pint plastic bottle. It is transparent and contains blackcurrant juice. A transparent or orange opaque tube leads from its top. She cradles the white figure and pushes the end of the tube through a hole in the hood. It feeds. She nurses it and tidies its clothes.*

A Story

TRENCH. Mankind through the ages. A clown with a gun. An idiot with a stick. Little men plotting in tiny corners. Hunting for a uniform to cover themselves in. Or a mob to hang on to. The human species. Homo mob. Have you seen it? I saw it once. Screaming. One of the sounds it makes. The others are loud laughter and a muffled gibbering. I was abroad on a trade mission. I watched from the Hilton. They filled the square. There was a pedestal with a man on a horse on it. He was a general: he had a better uniform. The head was three feet across. It was smiling.

The mob threw ropes over it. Some of them climbed up and tied them on. An old man with a beard fell off. They dragged him away. Then the herd began to pull. 'Heave'. In their lingo but the meaning was clear. Heaving together. As if the sea was vomiting. Till it toppled and fell on them. There was blood. They broke it up with hammers and stones. They almost became quiet. The head came off. It was still smiling. They sawed off the horses legs. They pulled the man apart. The head rolled away into a corner of the square and smiled at them. When I came back a few years later there was a new statue on the pedestal. Of someone else. The new government was short of money. They had to use as much of the old statue as they could. Only the head was left. So they took it out of the corner of the square and stuck it on top of a new uniform. It was still smiling. Now you're here to change the world. Once upon a time. I don't hate you. One thing: your voice. The human voice still gives me pain. That's all. One day the world will be silent. Peace after the last shot.

*

ANNA *has finished feeding the* WHITE FIGURE *and put away the bottle.*

A Lecture

ANNA. Listen. There are two worlds. Most people think they live in one but they live in two. First there's the daily world in which we live. The world of appearance. There's law and order, right and wrong, good manners. How else could we live and work together? But there's also the *real* world. The world of power, machines, buying, selling, working. That world depends on capital: money! Money can do anything. It gives you the power of giants. The real world obeys the law of money. And there's a paradox about this law: whoever owns money is owned by it. A man buys a house. Does he own it? No, because to keep it he must get more money. He must obey the laws of money. And so the house owns him. The same is true of the clothes on your back and the food on your plate. Our lives, our minds, what we are, the way we see the world, are not shaped by human law but by the law of money. Behind our apparent freedom there's this real slavery. In the apparent world anyone can choose to be moral. But morality never touches the real world. Nothing is changed by the apparent 'good'. The real world follows its iron law. You understand? Let's see.

*

The Examination

We get rid of plagues and sickness, eat more, live in better houses, often we're less cruel, there are no executions. But at the same time things get worse. Vandalism, violence, fascism, weapons. Men run camps of mass murder and sing carols. So why is this paradox? Why is morality weak?

*

TRENCH *doesn't answer.* LISA *repeats the lecture.*

A Lecture Repeated

LISA. We live in two worlds. The real world of money controls the whole of the apparent world. Everything. Science, technology, work, education, law, morality, the press. Even us – our minds, our behaviour, the way we see the world: we're slaves unless we resist. That's why the world isn't human.

ANNA. As to the 'human mob'. We're not violent because

we're born with the need to hate. It's because instead of changing the real world we merely do good in this one. The earth can't hold two worlds anymore. It's too small. So we make the two worlds one. That's all revolution is: making the two worlds one. Making morality strong so that the real world will be changed. The morality of the world of appearance is too weak to do that. It's a matter of weapons. Using them causes suffering. But when appearance and reality are one there'll be less suffering. Men will know themselves – and the world will last in peace and prosperity.

*

LISA. Understand?

TRENCH. I didn't listen. I've heard it before. Better said. There *are* two worlds: your's and mine. We're in mine.

ANNA. There are the tools of the twentieth century: the machines, computers and bombs. Where are the ideas of the twentieth century? You can live – you can get fame and power – with the ideas of a stone-age hunter or a medieval fanatic. The ideas of the twentieth century are still not learnt!

TRENCH (*quietly. In his own world*). I try to stay awake. I don't want to sleep when the world ends. I want to see it end. The sky will turn bright. There'll be a roar. A great wind will blow open the windows and doors. Dust will come down on everything like a white sheet. It will blot out the horizon. I shall go blind. The world will begin to shrivel. A great noise will come from under the sheet. Then it will be silent.

A Confession

LISA (*staring through the window with binoculars*). I wish Michael was here. I want to get in the car and go. What will become of us? We'll always be hunted. In the end they'll get us.

ANNA. No. It will change.

LISA (*still staring through the binoculars*). Yes Anna. But after us. We have to pay. I'd've liked to have been an ordinary woman. Lived in a simple world. Loved Michael. Worked at what I wanted. Talked to the neighbours and children. The world isn't like that. It will be for our children. But I've only begun to live and now I could die.

*

ANNA. Well we chose.

A Fantasy

TRENCH. That white worm. Crawling along the floor. Food shoved up its hood. Led out to shit. Covered with a gun. What keeps it alive? A little thread of hope or cunning or hate or malice. It doesn't know the difference under the hood. Not that it matters. As long as it can dangle on it for a little time before it drops into the hole. If you took off its hood it would hang itself. That white corpse. That –

LISA (*at the window*). Car. (*She looks through binoculars.*) Michael.

ANNA (*collecting LISA's blanket*). That blanket.

LISA. Anna?

ANNA. What?

> ANNA *goes to the window. She takes* LISA's *binoculars. She looks through them.*

ANNA. He's driving too fast. Why's he driving so fast? (*Turns back to the room.*) Check his straps.

> LISA *checks the straps on the* WHITE FIGURE. ANNA *looks through the binoculars. The car is heard.*

ANNA (*binoculars*). He's alone.

LISA (*to* TRENCH *and the* WHITE FIGURE): One sound and I shoot.

ANNA (*binoculars. Under breath*). Don't hurry. Don't hurry. Don't hurry.

LISA. He's being chased.

ANNA (*binoculars*). The road's empty.

The car stops outside. ANNA *still looks from the window.*

MICHAEL (*off*). Anna! Anna!

ANNA (*to* LISA): Out of sight. It may be a trap.

LISA. But not if he –

ANNA. It may be a trap!

ANNA *and* LISA *hide.*

MICHAEL (*off*). Lisa!

ANNA. The bloody fool shouting our names!

MICHAEL *bursts into the room.*

MICHAEL. Lisa! Anna!

ANNA (*hidden*). Michael!

MICHAEL. HQ's busted. They must know this place. We've got to run. Quickly. (*Looks from the window.*) Quickly.

ANNA *and* LISA *come out of hiding.* ANNA *starts to pull the* WHITE FIGURE *to the door.*

ANNA. Help me.

MICHAEL (*looking through the window*). Leave that!

ANNA. We must –

MICHAEL (*looking through the window*). Leave it! No time! The car!

ANNA. What about the –

MICHAEL (*looking through the window*). We must move!

ANNA. A hostage is our only chance if we –

MICHAEL (*turns to* ANNA). Anna! No time!

LISA (*aims gun at* MICHAEL). It's a trap. Don't trust him.
MICHAEL. Please! Please!

They stare at each other.

ANNA. No Lisa. Go with him. I'll shoot it out. I'll cover you
from the porch.

> LISA *hesitates. Then lowers the gun. Goes out.* MICHAEL
> *follows her.*

MICHAEL (*off*). The hills.

> ANNA *picks up more ammunition. She goes out to the porch.*
> TRENCH *and the* WHITE FIGURE *are alone.* TRENCH
> *goes to it. Stoops. Undoes the straps on the legs. Goes to the
> picture. Hides behind it.*
> *The* WHITE FIGURE *staggers to its feet. It writhes to free
> its hands. It can't.*
> *Off, the sound of a helicopter.*
> *The* WHITE FIGURE *is terrified. It moves round the room
> to find a way out. It gets into the corridor.*
> *Off, the helicopter passes low overhead.*
> *The* WHITE FIGURE *panics. Tugs at the hood. It won't
> come off. Confuses the direction and returns to the room.
> Feels along the walls.*

HELICOPTER (*off*). Drop your arms. Face down on ground.
Arms stretched out. Hands flat to ground.

> *The* WHITE FIGURE *writhes. Frees one hand. Tugs at the
> hood. It won't come off. It flays round with its free hand.
> Tugs at hood again. It comes off. The chauffeur is blinded
> by the light. Peers. Staggers. Sees picture.* TRENCH'*s head
> is in the hole. Chauffeur tries to speak. No sound.* TRENCH
> *pushes his hand through the canvas. It holds a pistol.*
> TRENCH *shoots. The chauffeur is killed.* TRENCH *stares at
> him from the hole in the canvas. The pistol smokes.*
> *Off, sounds of helicopters, cars, police dogs.*

HELICOPTER (*off*). Remove your clothes. Throw items well clear. Girl first.

SIX

Park.
TERRY, JOHN *and* BERYL *on a bench. A pram.*

BERYL. All this for a few measly quid. No wonder it take so long to change anythin.

JOHN. It'll pay for a proper holiday. If I don't get one I'm knackered for the rest of the year.

BERYL. There'll be a whip round for his wife.

JOHN. Who reckons the lads'll jack it in?

BERYL. The papers'll have a go. Not nice when you're called an animal. The kids read it.

JOHN. Bet Ray's havin a go.

BERYL. Non-stop. What'll we tell the papers?

TERRY. When?

BERYL. When they ask what we think now he's dead. They're bound to ask.

JOHN. We didn't know they'd kill him.

BERYL. We said take the risk.

JOHN. Anyway it was only the dead girl. The other two were in custody.

BERYL. What'll we say?

Press Release

TERRY. 'Militants condemn terror.' So everyone's still got their right label. We can go home happy. What good's that? If you're ignorant that's your excuse. But if you know what sort of world you're in you have to change it.

Well what world is it? The poor are starving. The rich are gettin ready to blow it up. Terrorists threaten with guns? We do it with bombs. One well-heeled American with his finger on the button. That's sick. And there's worse than that. The ignorance we live in. We don't understand what we are or what we do. That's more dangerous than bombs. We're all terrorists. Everyone of us. We live by terror. Not even to make a new world: just to keep one that's already dead. In the end we'll pay for that as much as the lot who're starvin now.

How long can we go on like this? Yet we sit here as if we had all the time in the world. All of us: we sit.

When they ask me to condemn terror I shall say: no. *You* have no right to ask. You are a terrorist.

*

The Activists Papers

Memorandum
A Fallacy
Learning
The Theft of a Bun
Song of the Top Policeman
The Team
Speaking with Actors
Advice to Actors
On Working with Young Actors
A Rehearsal in the Garage
A Note to Young Writers
Antigone
The Simple Image
On Weapons
The New Fascism
The Struggle for Reason
A Story
Those Who Go Before
The Thinkers
On Violence
Types of Drama
On Texture
If We Were Here
The Art of the Audience
A Poem
On Aesthetics
On Problems

The Activists Youth Theatre Club is part of the Royal Court Theatre's Young People's Theater Scheme. Most of The Activists Papers were written when I rehearsed *The Worlds* with them.

A Fallacy, *Learning* and *The Theft of a Bun* were written while I rehearsed the play with students at Newcastle University. Earlier versions of *A Note to Young Writers* and *The Art of the Audience* were written for the Warehouse company of the Royal Shakespeare Company.

The papers are an introduction to the play. Extracts from them may be printed in theatre programmes. They need not be read in the order in which they are printed here.

MEMORANDUM

The word reason alienates many people. Especially in universities. They think of it as being inhuman and cold. They think of theatre and the other arts as being human and warm.

We live and relate to ourselves, others, technology and our environment by organizing our behaviour and consciousness, with its attitudes and concepts, into a society. These things interconnect and mutually form one another. By 'rational' I mean the condition that exists when this is done in such a way that we're as sane and behave as morally and humanely as historically possible at that time. All societies should desire this state of affairs. Few do. In most societies it's assumed that when technological change (from the stone axe-head to the electronic computer) creates new wealth and new ways of using resources and abilities, these things should be fitted into the existing social order. So the consciousness and beliefs of the members of society are arranged so as to make this possible. I say arranged and not manipulated because it's not likely to be done by conspiracy. It's not even likely to be done consciously. This makes it harder to detect and describe. The ruling class doesn't know what it's doing. That's why it's always losing its temper.

There are two grounds on which the ruling class justifies its obstruction of rational change. First it maintains law and order. It sees this as synonymous with maintaining decent social relations. But social relations are based on a particular social order. In time if this order doesn't change it becomes unjust. The ruling class denies this. Its second ground is that it's better washed, better mannered, better dressed and is interested in cultural affairs that are far superior to mere labour and survival. In a word, it protects the best. It sees people in the working class as being almost animals.

It sees itself as being synonymous with civilization and its cultivation as coming from its natural abilities and not from its wealth and privileged opportunities. It doesn't see that the way in which it monopolizes these things distorts the culture it derives from them and that this makes its culture irrational and an enemy of civilization.

To keep society as it is the ruling class uses education, media, jobs, bribes, punishments and other means of informing, commenting and persuading to make people think and behave in ways that will justify its rule. It doesn't fight the bad with the good, it uses both in an infernal alliance. This means that when it acts moral distinctions break down. Clearly almost any good action can be used to corrupt and damage. Charity may support a system that impoverishes. Teaching may strengthen ignorance. What has to be understood is that the ruling class uses every means it can to create social conditions and attitudes that will justify its claim to maintain law and order. Guilt, greed, envy, sexual repression, public disorder, self-denigration ('we're all animals'), everything that turns men back to their past – these are its cultural foundations. Its claim to represent justice depends on its ability to create injustice.

Here is an example to do with education. People are educated according to their class and money. Rich parents can buy their stupid children the best education. The stupid children of the poor get the worst. But society must at least appear just so the bright children of the poor may be sent to the schools of the rich. Earlier this century a man who ran an almost feudal estate sent two bright boys to university every year. This disguised his despotism as enlightenment. An apparently good action was used to strengthen a bad system. This is the point: the bright boys had to behave themselves – and so did their parents. It also took possible malcontents away from their natural allies. The working class is often clannish. Even now getting above your station may be risky if it exposes you and your friends. Employers (as once the gentry) can pick you out more easily. In this way intelligence is a danger to the community. This attitude can only change when the working class can properly educate and support all its members.

Our relationships are based not only on beliefs and ideas but also on emotions. That is very useful to a ruling class. Emotions are effected by both the mind and the body. The first is easier to understand and so I'll say something about the second. A drowning man is afraid and may panic. A man resting in the sun is likely to be at peace. All the while we react to our environment in this way. Housing, factories, streets, the organization of work, the amount and security of wages, all these things, the physical, institutional, legal, domestic environment – in a word the social environment – effect our emotions. If the social environment isn't one that helps us to live humanely (socialism) but helps in our exploitation (capitalism) or makes us beasts or machines (fascism) then our emotions tend to deteriorate into fear, tension and racial and religious paranoia which lead to aggression, vandalism, child battering and other forms of violence. By education and information in newspapers, films, entertainment and so on the ruling class stresses this condition and reinforces it with pseudo-science and folky mythology. Mind and emotions prey on themselves and on each other. Ideas become infested with illusions and myths. Men behave in ways which aren't based on the world they're in but on the one they believe they're in. This is irrational and when we're irrational our condition deteriorates. Fear and tension aren't static conditions. Irrationalism leads to increasing hysteria, paranoia, apathy and violence and so society declines. In this way capitalism uses law and order to capitalize on the damage it does to men. It claims that a destructive emotional state is part of 'human nature' – as is its final consequence, war. This is what passes for its culture. It's the commentary we live by. Surely to those who come after us it will seem madness?

As technology changes so the society and behaviour based on the earlier technology becomes unable to use the new technology properly. Industrial and social relations break down. Technology makes the old society unworkable and the old society can't change itself so as to make the new technology work. Nevertheless it must try to make it work: so Hitler buys a plane and goes electioneering. If you don't make society and consciousness more rational then they must become more irrational. As technology changes *they* can't remain the same. The aggressive emotional condition and the behaviour it provokes must become more irrational and violent. To combat this the ruling class becomes even more coercive, its culture more decadent and its view of human nature more pessimistic. This aggravates the condition it's supposed to prevent. After all, it's only a more extreme form of the reaction that created the condition in the first place. But the ruling class can't understand what's happening or what it's doing. That's why comparative affluence failed to make the West more civilized.

The decline has no set pattern. Variation is almost infinite. Lies and excuses give way to new lies and new excuses. Perhaps the ruling class claims that it's civilized and the working class is brutal. Or it may argue racially. The working class is brutal but less brutal than even the elite of another race. Or it may say this of a social group. Often it's created the group itself: vandals for example. Or it claims that it has all the managerial skills and so we must all support it for the common good. And so on.

Our ability to be irrational is the necessary condition but not the cause of fascism. Hitler came to power because the German economy broke down. Money was devalued and there was poverty and unemployment. But affluence doesn't prevent fascism. In itself affluence doesn't make society rational, it merely gives fascism a new form. An irrational society projects its irrationality into individuals in many ways. I've described only some of them. Unless technological, industrial, economic and political relationships – unless all relationships involving human beings – are rational or developing rationally, then they produce fascism. I say 'rational or developing rationally' because we should use 'reason' to describe either a rational state or its creation. The word culture should be used in the same way: to mean a state of culture or – the only possibility open to us – the struggle for it.

The struggle for rationalism is of course against irrationalism. That's why it may have to be violent. If it is violent then superficially it seems itself to be irrational. Nevertheless the growth of rationalism can be seen in history. There are two reasons why its growth may be unclear. Partly, as I've said, it's because of the nature of the struggle: rationalism may have to use irrational means. And partly it's because as the irrationalism of the old order dwindles advances in technology give greater power to what's left of it. If you wish to see the growth of reason in history consider this. What would a medieval pope armed with H-bombs have done to infidels if he believed (as he did) that if he spared them suffering in this world they'd suffer for eternity in the next – and so would he?

Irrational society can't reform itself or stay as it is. Neither force nor fear can save it. Nor can its attempts at tolerance, kindness or charity. As we've seen, it corrupts moral action and whatever force it uses must hasten its end. The social order is itself irrational and would collapse into barbarism if there were not rational forces at work in it. These forces are the forces of socialism. They change the relationships between the classes and therefore the society and culture based on them. Socialism is caused by the collapse of the old society and is a cause of its collapse. The collapse of the old society and the creation of the new are aspects of the same

historical event. The old society wouldn't collapse if socialism wasn't necessary. Socialism is the working of reason and
the foundation of human culture. What is at stake is the
human mind.

A FALLACY

Whether the stomach is full or empty
Whether the house is large or small
All men are equal in joy or pain
There's only one sound of laughter
One sound of tears
And all who go in darkness stumble
In the calamity small differences are swept away
Men are united in common suffering
Master and servants weep at the grave

And it's true that all hungry men
Reach for the plate with one appetite
But not that all men have enough to eat
Or that the old man wrapped in linen
And the thin youth shot on the square
Should be mourned with the same cry
Humanity isn't shared when the rest is shared unjustly
Yet the hypocrites go on braying
All men are brothers!
As if that were the password of thieves

LEARNING

In the House of Preliminary Detention
By copying letters from cigarette packets
The worker and socialist revolutionary
Nikolay Vasilyev taught himself to read

He then got books and using his new knowledge
Wrote in capital letters
'MR PROSECUTOR DEAR SIR I AM THROWN IN THIS
  HOLE
FOR NO REASON
WITHOUT LIGHT OR AIR OR SPACE OR THE COMPANY
  OF PEOPLE
HAVE YOU NO GOD?'

There was no answer
One night he heaped the books over himself
Set them on fire and burned to death

From this there's much to learn
When knowledge is taught by the ignorant
We should fear not only the burners of books
We should fear the builders of libraries

THE THEFT OF A BUN

When the boy runs from the shop
Into the arms of a priest who says
'It's wrong to steal'
He turns white and drops the bun in the street

He doesn't ask the priest why it's wrong to steal
So the priest needn't answer
'Christ shed his blood on the cross
For the three-in-one-and-one-in-three
To redeem sinners except those elected by god
To be damned...'

The priest would be speaking long after the bun was stale
Even when it had turned to stone

But the boy doesn't ask because
The priest has one word that stands for many
This is the way lies may pass unquestioned

If we'd answered we'd have said
'It's wrong to steal
But if you're starving it may not be wrong
Ask why you steal
Ask is the owner a thief?'

And then we'd need to use so many words
The spectators would have gone home to dinner
Long before we'd finished
That's why truth often disperses a crowd
And is met walking alone and is jeered at
She doesn't have one word for many

SONG OF THE TOP POLICEMAN
(*To sad music*)

In the old days when I was young I slogged the beat
I passed the time by picking pockets
Nothing like it in the gentle summer sun
Lifting wallets in broad daylight on the street
Some days I made a ton
Now I sit behind a desk
You can't hear a truncheon drop the carpet is so deep
And it's all taking bribes from villains on the make or toffs
  who made it
They pass it over with a handshake and I go back to sleep
Of course I'm grateful for the dough
But the fun's gone out of life as I knew it long ago

In the old days the good old days when I was young I slogged
    the beat
When I was bored with clear blue skies and sun
I'd run a blackie up a sidestreet and drop him in the doorway
    of a shop
Then put the boot in and make the bastard hop – well you
    need a bit of fun
When the rent's behind and you're quarrelling with the wife
My panting mingling with the laddie's screams
Brought back fond memories of my brief boyhood
When we played pirates by laughing sunlit streams
Now the fun has really gone out of my life

I sit alone in my big office thumbing catalogues of guns
Sometimes there's an exhibition of riot gear and tear gas
(One lad went on crying even after I'd hammered in his skull
    – it's top-notch stuff)
But I haven't seen a decent bit of action not since years
Never hear a bone crack or a yell as the lads wade in with riot
    sticks
In worldly terms I'm doing very well out of the reach of flying
    bricks
But all the same my life is very dull

THE TEAM

The dogs dragged the sledge over the ice. It was hard work.
Perhaps it was even harder for the explorer. He wasn't used
to the cold. Fortunately he didn't have to waste strength
whipping the dogs. They obeyed his voice. In camp at night
they were let out of harness and fed. After feeding they didn't
run away. They were tired. They slept. And there was
nothing to eat out in the snow. In the morning they were
strapped into the harness. The order was given. 'Mush!'

Young dogs don't run away from their mother. And when the trainer takes them they're kept in a pen. If a dog is lured away by the dark green forest he's caught and beaten. The trainer has a secret – or rather a knack, because he doesn't understand it himself. He teaches the dog to train itself. Even when the trainer's dead the dog carries him in his head. This isn't to say that dogs become men but that sometimes a man becomes a dog.

Dogs know that meat doesn't spring from the ground. Still, the explorer had meat in tins. Surely this was manna from heaven? His dogs believed he was god. That's why they worked for him.

God was overdue. He was lost. So he used the whip. He made the working day longer. There weren't many tins left. Even now the dogs stayed with him. They trusted him. He wasn't wantonly cruel. In the good times he hadn't used the whip. Besides, what else could they do? They were famished and tired. They worked as best they could and did what they were told.

One night a dog tried to slink away. God tied him to the sledge and whipped him. Afterwards he left him tied there. He lay in the snow beside the sledge and slept. In the night he whimpered in his sleep. In the morning he was dead. God stripped the carcass. He cooked and ate some of the good meat. He packed the rest in snow in a sack. He tied the sack onto the sledge. He threw the offal, hide and bones to the dogs.

Two nights later the dogs were still hungry after their meal. They quarrelled. God cowed them with his whip. Then he put them in the harness. They spent the night in it.

God went on with his journey. He travelled under the bright stars. Slowly the weather turned. The strong wind came. Steadily the temperature fell. God ran out of tins. Now the dogs lived in the harness. From time to time one was taken out and killed. That's how god fed himself and his dogs. Each time he killed a dog the dogs that were left pulled the sledge more slowly. God's face darkened. A dull light shone in his eyes. He cracked the whip as if he were dancing. He believed they were moving fast. If you'd watched from a hill you'd have seen the team crawl over the ice as slowly as a worm. Now the dogs were imprisoned in the harness. Otherwise they would have run away. The cold killed the last two dogs and the explorer. His body lay on the lee side of the sledge. The dogs lay in the harness.

We should be sorry for these poor creatures. The circumstances of their deaths were as absurd as their lives. But don't be greatly worried. Men are neither gods nor dogs.

SPEAKING WITH ACTORS

He writes a cheque
That only proves he's in cash
Does the mother hold the child because she's kind?
Wait!
The mother can't waste kindness on that
She holds it because it will fall
Kindness is a special thing
Only those who run in the street are kind
They drag their fallen friend to the doorway

Was this soldier merciful?
How can I know? His uniform won't tell me
All I know is he's dead
To learn how to kill he shot at targets
They told him 'be proud of your uniform'
No one told him it was only a target
Why do they wear targets?
It would be a kindness to tell them
You'd be arrested

Don't let's sit and talk of the good
Not even the air's good here
You actors! don't crawl on the stage and question your soul
If it hasn't already answered you're wasting our time
And don't tell us you have problems
We know the problems
But you act opening the door and forget to look in the room
Open your eyes as you go through the doorway
Then we see that you understand problems

You act what's happening
Only the dead do that and nothing much happens to them
Something's going to happen
Now that's interesting!
Where will we be in an hour?
What will we do next year?
As you sit at rest in the chair
Show us that next year you'll run for your life in the street
As you do one thing let us see in it what you'll do next
As we see what you are let's see in it what you'll become
Act what's going to happen and what you will be
How else can you act what you are?

It's not that you don't interest us
But when we know what interests you you're more
    interesting
Unless all that interests you is yourself

All our characters must be Lear Hamlet Cordelia and Helen
But that's only a start
Much more is happening
Lear sits in a corner and you're the storm
Is there peace when the storm dies?
No
Lear cried for justice and you have to give it
So act what's going to happen

ADVICE TO ACTORS

Actors
Don't try to make your character possible
Men do things that ought not to be possible
Don't say 'he'd never do this'
Men don't behave in expected ways
Don't make the character one man
Unfortunately a man is many men
Don't worry when an action isn't consistent
Men aren't consistent
Ask why they're not consistent
Find out the uncharacteristic in a character
Find out why the character stops being himself
In this world we're still not human
Some try to be human
Others are butchers or worse
Start work again when you say 'he'd never do this'
You may be close to understanding
Why this man seeks freedom and that man's a butcher

Don't search for a soul
A soul won't help you to understand what's done
It's a white rabbit pulled from a hat when the truth's hard to
    follow
It's not a motive for acting truth
Don't try to become the character
That's impossible and if you try you give up responsibility for
    what you do
You give up judgement and without it you can't create
Possess the character don't let it possess you
Take your life to what the writer offers as useful
Acting changes the written word and the described gesture
As much as wind changes the shapes of clouds and clothes

Words change as you speak them and again as they're heard
Without these changes the play is a paper ghost

The character is by nature angry or happy?
How little this tells us!
The SS guard and the inmate are happy
There's not one anger or one happiness or one courage
But there is only one justice
The SS guard is happy
Emotions don't make us human
It's not even true to say that virtuous acts make us good
Judge by the situation not by the character or his actions
A starving prisoner gives a child bread
The guard gives it bread
He knows tomorrow the child will be gassed
Is the guard kind? He's mad
But it's still an act of kindness?
No it's an act of madness
The same act has many meanings
There's no soul common to all men
All that we have in common is reason and some men use
    reason to defend madness
So show us the situation
Then we can see how vices and virtues
May pass through our minds under false names
As a man smiles when a pistol is in his back
Or a man disguises himself at the frontier post
You ask is he a bandit or friend of the people?
Don't expect his disguise to tell you!

A miner finds gold in the hills
He changes his clothes and eats well
You act this but what have you taught us?
Go to the hills!
The poor are still poor

The past still hides the past and the future is still uncertain
For shame! Why waste our time?
Don't show us a man who comes to terms with this world
His life isn't changed – only his way of life
There's nothing for you to act in that
The miner's nails are clean – that's all you act!

The fishwife is clever or stupid
You show which but you still haven't shown us the fishwife
The cleverness of the fishwife and her customer aren't the
    same
There's not one cleverness
The cleverness that makes the fishwife cunning
May make her customer a good mother
The fishwife can't be shown by her character
Her life's shaped by the stall
By the storm that blows on the quay
Till the canvas over her head flaps like a vulture's wings
By the sun that makes the fish stink when the passersby are
    too poor to buy
By hauling baskets and haggling with skippers
By speaking at the stall holders' meeting
By bribing the licensing officer
By all the business of selling and buying fish

Two lovers alone in a room
One leaves the bed and puts on his brown tunic
Two more lovers in some other room
One weeps
We don't share one love
You can't show a girl in a kitchen till you show us the landlord
And who runs the city
The clock stands at three
You can't tell the time till you know the century

A man tends the rosetrees in his garden
The city is run by gangsters
He builds a high wall round his garden to shut out the urchins
Who sees the beautiful roses?
The gangsters kill him behind his wall
Who sees the killers?

What does the character bring to his situation?
Characteristics? Temperament? Useless!
Is he proud? Of what? Angry? When? Kind? To whom?
Unless we know a man's situation we can't say if he's good or
evil
How can the fishwife fix the price of fish till she knows the
state of the market?
How can she know what she does till she knows what world
she's in?
The pessimism of one man and the optimism of his neighbour
May change the world in the same way
What should a man understand? His life
That is his situation and what he does in it
His life isn't made by what he does to himself
It's made by what he does to his situation
The SS guard doesn't understand his life
You will act many men who don't understand their life
Not all wear uniforms to warn us
So how important that *you* understand!

It's clear a character can't be acted
You must act a life
I repeat a character can't be acted
This is a paradox but true
The parable of the leaf and sail will help you to understand
A leaf driven before a storm sought its tree
It called to the wind for help

But the strongest storm can't blow one leaf back onto its tree
On the lake a boat raises its sail
It takes the wind and crosses the sea
It can even make port in the teeth of the storm
The character can be compared to the leaf
What you should act can be compared to the sail
What you call character is only self
The self does nothing but call to the storm
The life of one man is explained by the lives of all men
You don't need to understand his character
You need to understand his life
You need a way to show this understanding
A man is either himself or all men
You must act all men
That is the theatre of reason
Act this understanding
Act learning
Don't reproduce – don't call the wind
Judge!
Let your playing show that you understand history
The changes that men make and that make men

The acting of knowledge is like a window
Of good proportion and clear glass
To show us the world
We bring the audience to the window
They see how they live
And how others have lived before them and made this world
And how they can remake it
This is of great use but it's not drama
This is drama:
'Man the seeker and finder of knowledge'
That men seek and when they find what is true they know it
That's why they're called men
That is the ancient lure that brings them to the stage

Cattle go to the pool to quench thirst
They drink and their thirst is quenched
Men go to the pool and drink with their parched throat
But they're not quenched till they see their face in the water
That's why they're called men
They see they are men who seek understanding
Oedipus is both foolish and wise
Knowledge is truth but not art
In art there's always justice
In drama the meaning of justice is clear
In drama man learns who he is

We also show that men question truth
We know things that to our forefathers were secret
But they sought!
Their plays bear the scars of reason and are among the classics
We have new weapons and tools of understanding
Justice is no longer the cry of the falsely accused
Justice is passed on the false accusers
In your acting guide us in our changing times
Show justice
And we shall know her when she comes to meet us on the
    street

ON WORKING WITH YOUNG ACTORS

The stage is the court of justice herself
Some players play in the masks they wear off-stage
They're like the curteous men in striped suits
Who step from the pavement to let evil pass
Don't learn their tricks!
When an actor goes onto the stage he shows what he lives for

How else could he act other men's lives?
And there's justice in this
The way you judge them is the way you judge yourself

Actors! understand that each word and gesture shows why
    you live
We don't hear the human voice but the human brain
When you speak you show us all that's in your mind
Remember the distance between the brain and the voice
Is the longest way in the world
Did you die on the way?
What is this stranger saying? In what tongue?
How can we understand – he can't even tell us where he came
    from?
Well who has something to say?
Those who watch and listen
And speak when silence would make them
Accomplices to the crime

Lies too need time to grow
But perhaps you've already run on ahead
To lay traps and snares on your way
In time you'll meet yourself
Waiting on corners and sitting in strange rooms
Offering yourself coins or a knife
Or in too much despair to look up as you enter
Already some of these meetings have been arranged

Then how will you live? What can you do?
Work for evil or good
Nothing else can be done with your life
No other choice
The stage shows how you choose
Help us to choose
Choose well

A REHEARSAL IN THE GARAGE

If you were learning to kill they'd give you weapons
Hot food a uniform and a dry hall

Their pals give you bright lights and music
That's why they give you money
So they can rob you
Sure! you need to dance
And who dances better?
But they grab everything
They'll leave you nothing

We work in the cold garage till eleven at night
When you came you were tired
From carrying bricks and studying primers
Rain weeps through the ceiling
But listen how joyfully it's hammering on the roof!
Wind comes through each hole in the wall
Is it that curious to see what we're doing?
It must be interesting!
When we work the world tries to burst in
Those others, they're trying to shut it out

A NOTE TO YOUNG WRITERS

Perhaps every twenty years there will be a new generation of
angry young writers. They'll have a right to be angry.
There'll still be many things to be angry about. But what use
is it that five times in a century young writers tell us they're
angry? Anger may be caused by impotence.

We haven't done much when we've abused the stupid and
presumptuous people in power. Abuse won't take away their

power. And it's not enough merely to point out where their misuse of it leads. We must say how they got it and how they keep it.

Capitalism needs to understand the nature of things. It uses science to do this. It doesn't want to understand people. Such an understanding would destroy the deception on which it bases its confidence. It would also make it easier for the people it controls to understand themselves. This would make them harder to control. Capitalism doesn't want to know what we are but merely how we can be manipulated. To this end it creates a mythology about men and society. This passes for its culture – and it's almost feudal.

When capitalist culture controls science and technology we're in danger. Dramatists are right to warn of an apocalypse. But that's only part of the truth. Capitalism doesn't have to lead either to a stable fascist state or to the end of the world. That sort of pessimism is irrational.

Capitalism sees men as bestial. They must be restrained by law and order and manipulated by incentive and coercion. This is its image of man. It's mythological. But it can't free itself from this mythology. To do that it would have to stop being capitalism. That's why capitalism can never again be fit to control science and technology. It uses them irrationally. It's rational only about things and the way they work. It's not rational about men or their relation to things or to each other. In other words capitalism no longer expresses reality in an adequate and accurate way. It no longer has a culture.

Capitalism uses education and morality to teach men lies about themselves and society. It starts doing this when they're children and that's one reason why the teaching has an effect. But men have no lasting need to believe lies. Indeed, the lies they are taught go against their daily experience. For many reasons all men try, sometimes more and sometimes less, to express their experience in an adequate and accurate way – that is, rationally. In a time of capitalist irrationalism a rational culture can be created only by the expression of working class experience, and the working class must obviously take the major part in creating it. This rational culture will need new political and social forms. It will also need a new image of men and women – and new artistic forms to create it. Writers can create art only by working to create this culture. It's the only way they can record the truth. Writers who don't help to do this peter out in silence or hide their increasing superficiality under deeper obscurantism or run for the bolt-hole of reaction. Contemporary theatre has examples of all three.

The form of the new drama will be epic. This name is often misunderstood, partly because the form isn't yet fully developed. An epic play tells a story and says why it happened. This gives it a beginning, a middle and an end joined together in a truthful way. This isn't true of the theatre of the absurd. It sees life as meaningless: it has a beginning and an end but no middle. The bourgeois theatre is concerned only with anecdotes: they have a middle but no beginning and end.

Epic plays don't need to cover centuries or have a cast of armies. The essence of epic theatre is in the way it selects, connects and judges. Even when it deals with two people quarrelling in a kitchen it draws its method and values from the understanding of the history of all men. How else should you judge between right and wrong? Bourgeois writers believe that only they write with subtlety and sensitivity. They see epic theatre as abstract, inhuman and cold. But what they call subtle and sensitive is only arbitrary and incomplete. They try to derive meaning from the incidental. No, the broad structure of history must be understood before the incidents in it can be given meaning. That's why the epic is the only form of theatre that can be subtle and sensitive – and have good taste, wit, nuance and human intimacy.

Bourgeois theatre lacks this sense of purpose and this makes it inhuman. It would be unfair to judge its subtlety and sensitivity on the fodder it gives to tired businessmen and their bored clients. That would let it off very lightly. It ought to be judged on the crudity, shallowness and vulgarity of the plays admired by its intellectuals.

Anger and apocalypse aren't enough. Theatre must talk of the causes of human misery and the sources of human strength. It must make clear how and why we live in a culture of nihilism. And because the understanding of history has been contaminated with mythology it must rewrite it to make sense of the future. To do these things we need a rational theatre.

ANTIGONE

In the old plays kings fought kings
Quarrelled with princes and queens
And told the people when to take the leather tool-bag
From the worn skin of their shoulder
And strap on the knapsack
Because in those days power went to the kings
And as art deals with justice
It told how the kings used power

The king took the people's power
His small hand was a giant's
It sent ministers from the room
And drove armies into mud on the broken banks of the river
If his mood was bad he sat down with sycophants in a corner
    to corrupt justice
His family quarrel was the state quarrel
His fate was the people's fate
Because power went to the kings

And whether Antigone or Creon is right
Is a question that has no answer
How can a man of power be human?
How can he use his power for good?
Antigone and Creon are vultures who fight for a corpse after
    battle
Antigone's screams can't tell us
The meaning of justice

Men with great power don't govern a human state
They take the people's power but can't take their wisdom
When the people have lost their power
Their wisdom is lost to the state
Those without power are without wisdom
And the people who say it's right that the king should take
    our power
Will be wrong in all matters of law and justice that follow
As much as a man who can't tell you the day he was born
Can't tell you his age

All giants are tyrants
No tyrant is human
If Creon has power he can't be just
And Antigone's weakness can't make her wise
Or her pain teach her the law
But the people who know their right to power
Are wise in all that follows
Then power itself is wise
And the wound that divided power from justice is healed
So that the human smile is stronger than armies
That once roamed on the face of the earth
Then we'll know how to bury our dead
And how to live

THE SIMPLE IMAGE

In the time of the hand-held plough
Of kings in purple and gold
And inquisition into the mind
When the poor woman served her children
Bread at the scrubbed wooden table
The bread was pure and her smile without guilt
And her hands were clean
Because she worked in a field that wasn't stolen
And though her husband rused like a raddled fox
He was honest and stole only what had been stolen from him
And at play his children sang in joy of the world

And now in the time of bombs
And troops in the drab overalls of mass executioners
And inquisition into the mind
When bad bread is served from a plastic bag
On the formica top of a plastic table
To a man who works in armaments
And to children who sing commercial jingles
Where shall we find the simple image of truth?

The family is still exploited
Still suffer all that follows
When the mind's coerced for profit
And is not free to create a decent life among neighbours
There's still unemployment and debt
The crime of all preying on all fills prisons
Hospitals are full of sick in body and mind
Education is superstition
And morals are fraud and violence
That's still how we live

Don't be misled
The exploiter tells cynical tales
In schools he teaches despair
His theatre shows the slave's mind as enslaved
He fears the truth because the exploited speak it
In his language only lies can be spoken

In the simple house in the east quarter
Mind isn't formed by money
Or character by hiring and selling
Instead hand and brain work together
And the brain sees what the hand does
So that the value of all things can be seen
There you'll find the simple image of truth

The woman who watches at night by the sickbed
Not reading the open book on her lap
The care of the father who serves at the table
The children's mouths as they hold out their plate
The frown of the anxious mother as she enters the shop
In all these things there is beauty
And beauty always gives warning of storm
Of change
There is the simple image of truth

ON WEAPONS

It's in the nature of things that we have buses before we know
how to ride in them, cars before we know how to drive them
and spades before we know how to dig with them. We have
machines before we know how to use them because at first we
don't know all that they do. A machine doesn't merely make a
glass or a shoe. Those who make and use the machine are

changed by it. It doesn't give them a new purpose but it makes it necessary for them to live in a new way. Machines demythologize the earth, men and their societies. They make the old expression of humanity, and the old society connected with it, inhuman. All technology changes us and our society. It changes the way we live and so our beliefs, attitudes, customs, behaviour, consciousness itself – all change. And as consciousness is both mental and emotional the change in us is great enough to make us different people. We become either more rational or more irrational.

Our species innovates. When we change the mechanical means by which we live we have to change our social relation-ships. We develop new attitudes to the rest of society and what's in our heads changes. In the business of maintaining ourselves we change ourselves. How else could we co-operate in new ways? And how can society work without co-operation – either forced, as in the past, or freely as is made possible and necessary by modern technology? There's a constant mutual influence between technology, the human mind and social order. Society changes so that it can use its new machines and the users of new machines change so that they can use them and live in the new society. If we're to remain human these changes must be rational. In fact it's by making these changes rationally that we create our humanity. Each generation inherits its humanity from its society but it retains it only by recreating it in solving its new problems. That's what human-ity is: each generation is faced with new problems and in solving them it creates its new humanity. Obviously feudal society couldn't run modern technology. But more import-ant, if we try to run modern technology on the consciousness and social relations of feudalism we don't get feudalism. Instead what are now irrational social relations distort con-sciousness in order to bridge the gap between the old social order and the consciousness made necessary by the working of new technology. That distortion is fascism.

A weapon is a machine for causing respect, fear, pain or death. It has a good and a bad use. What good use? When technology changes human consciousness, social change is also necessary. Society resists change. It's based on laws and property relations that benefit the rulers of the old social order. They run it on the old form of consciousness calcified in universities, churches, theatres, customs, opinions and so on. We live in societies that are both new and old and which are therefore unsuited to many of our needs. If a society isn't changed rationally then the consciousness of many people in it is distorted so that they become, in effect, less human. Many resist this distortion but even so rational change is often late. It can't always be brought about by peaceful persuasion. Every day men learn the ways in which society doesn't meet human needs but they may not understand how much must change before it can meet them. Perhaps it seems a few small changes will do. But often small needs amount to vast social desires. For all to eat well there must be liberty and governments have had to fall before children could wear shoes. Society can't be just and rational in part. What we do and are depend on the relationships between everyone in society. The force and mythology needed to hold together an unjust society damage everything in it.

From time to time the conflict between society and the new needs and new consciousness of the people in it falls into crisis. Then the old society is destroyed by force. This is revolution. That is the good use of weapons. They're used to create a society in which consciousness doesn't have to be distorted and our needs can be met in a human way. It's not merely a struggle to take power and wealth from some and give it to others, it's a struggle (as we see) for the freedom of the human mind to express its humanity. Power and wealth in the hands of the old rulers dehumanizes society. It must be put into new hands before we can recreate humanity. So it's easy to see why change comes late. Revolutions aren't caused by those who desire them but by those who don't, by those who lose not those who gain by them. Many who read this will be against revolution and many of them will be the cause of revolution. This paradox shows the irrational way we still run our affairs. It's why reason still has to use irrational means.

Not all revolutions serve reason. Often the old society uses revolution to attack the new consciousness. It captures the new technology and tries to use it to drive men back to their past. Think of Hitler's electioneering planes and the death factories that came later. Fortunately totalitarianism must perish in a machine age. Superficially it seems that machines might help it (1984) but they only help it to get power not to keep it. Totalitarianism conflicts with the needs of the new consciousness created by technology. A modern totalitarian society becomes increasingly irrational and as a result unworkable. It can only tolerate the violence and hysteria needed to keep it going by apathy – and this makes it even more unworkable. In a modern totalitarianism the trains wouldn't run on time. It would bleed to death internally or if like Hitler's Germany it tried to save itself by going to war it would die of external wounds. It can't fight efficiently. A totalitarian soldier in a tank is as useless as a bushman handling a rifle for the first time. It's not that the soldier can't handle the tank efficiently but that his society can't. The only war a modern totalitarianism could wage efficiently would be total nuclear war – and it couldn't win that because it has no winner.

It's confusing to use the word revolution to describe the reactionary use of violence to save an old society. We should use it to describe only rational change. The confusion arises because in the past social change was studied in the universities, military academies and theological seminaries of the old societies. There all violent social change (even their own when they had to use it) was seen as bad because it disturbed the status quo. They classified by method not cause and this was misleading.

Affluence isn't an alternative to rational change. It makes that change more likely. It can't preserve an unjust society. Even a just society that was starving would have more chance of preserving itself. In an unjust society (and therefore in one which teaches, encourages and forces people to behave irrationally) the bribed can't trust the briber to go on paying. And anyway if the society is unjust the bribed will always want more. Really the briber is hostage to the bribed. Could there be a more absurd way of running our affairs? Affluence with socialism could bring peace, affluence without it must bring fascism. Affluence meets the needs only of an unjust society, or rather the needs it knows it has. Just societies need not only affluence but reason. Since western society doesn't understand this it can't do anything to get it. So it falls apart.

History needs weapons and revolutions. In time it won't. One day the old society will learn how to change peacefully into the new. But now it still clutches at power and tries to force its primitive forms onto our new, restless, changing world. It can neither work nor peacefully make way for the new. It produces discord, then reaction, then fascism. This delays rational change but it can't stop it.

THE NEW FASCISM

Technological and economic change make greater freedom possible and necessary. As human consciousness develops men demand more freedom. When they use more complicated machines, so that economic and social organization is made more elaborate, then as a rule they demand more autonomy. This is true even if their own job is simplified. It's enough for the machinery to be more complicated and the organization of the economy more complex. Men who accept more responsibility as workers or consumers demand more responsibility in the rest of their lives. Technological change destroys the old social structure, and the changing people construct a new one. They demand not just a society in which technology can work properly but one in which they can live together in decency. Unfortunately the demand can be corrupted. The old society tries to use technology and comparative affluence to cling onto power. This accelerates irrationalism, as we see, and leads to fascism. The fascism of affluence isn't the same as the fascism of poverty. The new fascism is the H-bomb, the mechanical Hitler. It's the product of irrationalism in affluent societies. Progress from scarcity to affluence doesn't make fascism impossible. It merely changes its form. Both forms may exist together.

Not only capitalist societies have H-bombs. Socialist societies have them. That's the ancient dilemma of good and evil. If reason could always choose its own weapons the history of man would have been different. Both capitalist and socialist societies have H-bombs but they're not both morally guilty for having them. Wherever technology is owned irrationally the production of H-bombs is likely and this makes their production necessary in societies which are becoming increasingly irrational. If technology is owned irrationally anywhere in the world then H-bombs will be made there and in many other societies.

Irrational societies create H-bombs. Irrational societies deteriorate through internal stress. It seems to follow that irrational societies must use their H-bombs. Affluence is as vulnerable before the new fascism as poverty is before the old. Socialism is the only alternative to fascism. On the road to hell there is no half-way house run by a liberal landlord. Socialism is the political definition of reason and without reason fascism grows.

THE STRUGGLE FOR REASON

The relationship between technology, consciousness and social order must be continually adjusted. This is in the nature of the relationship. History makes it increasingly possible for the relationship to be rational. As technology makes it possible for more and more people to become autonomous so the possibility of reason is made greater.

As the relationship between technology, consciousness and social order changes, so the relationships between workers, men and women, parents and children – all human relationships – change. If we make these changes rationally it doesn't mean that we lose our humanity, warmth, spontaneity, enjoyment and creativity – all those things which are the concern of art. Rationality isn't their enemy or even an alternative to them. They can't exist or be protected without it. Our wide use of technology to change our environment and our way of living has created problems in all human relationships. We've not yet solved these problems – and this is one reason why we misuse technology.

We use technology before we fully know what it does. When we use it we begin to live in new ways, create new experiences and gain new knowledge. We use all this to understand our new life and this understanding changes us again. All the time we behave differently and become different people. Each generation lives in a new world. Each generation must create its own humanity. If it's to be human it must develop new social relationships in which reason can flourish. Our minds can't be modern when we work and consume and feudal when we think and relate socially. Yet that's what capitalism demands. It brings chaos – the inarticulate cry for reason that can for a time be used to support the enemies of reason. Men long to be free of these ancient problems. With such burdens how can they live and work together in human decency? It's as if to free itself from the past our species always had to struggle for reason and cry for justice. That's what human societies do, that's what men are. Reason struggles in the whole world. Our lives invite us to reason and make it necessary. The cry for reason could only be stopped if we destroyed ourselves with nuclear weapons.

But before we can live in reason and justice – in accord – we must end the class order. Socialism makes the old idea of the classless brotherhood of man possible. It's the political working of reason. With it men can recreate their humanity in the time of advanced technology, even in the time of the H-bomb.

A STORY

The man-beast pulls the plough. If it pulls the plough in an orderly way the owner feeds it. The man-beast eats its fodder as all beasts might. If it's unruly the owner beats it. If it's dangerous he kills it.

A horse pulls the plough. The man-beast drives the horse. The man-beast learns he's not a beast. He's like the owner. The old rewards don't work. But the owner doesn't want to kill him. If he did who'd drive the horse? The man must be rewarded or punished in new ways. The owner tells him of heaven. He turns him into a religious-beast.

Next a tractor pulls the plough. The religious-beast drives the tractor. He also makes it. The owner owns the factory where the tractor's made. The religious-beast buys corn so that the owner makes a profit to invest in the factory to make the tractor. 'Wait a moment! I work for the boss so that he can make a profit to afford to hire me?' The man talks this over with the men who help him to make tractors. They ask the owner for more of the profit they make for him. The owner says no. The men stop work. They are many, the owner is one. It may be said that the men are masters but not owners.

Why isn't the factory working this morning? We could say that when the factory works the man pulls the plough and is driven by the horse. That's the easiest way to describe what happens when the master works for whoever he's master of.

Is this the modern world? Clearly it can't go on like this. What happens next? That depends. The master must become the owner. Then he'll be master of himself. Till then the horse goes on cracking the whip and calling him animal and nothing works.

THOSE WHO GO BEFORE

Machines changed our world and our minds
But we served the old ways
Things broke
Old customs and old beliefs – the old world itself
Didn't work
But we kept to the old ways

In change we saw only decay
The thin line of dawn was a blade at our throat
Roof tiles were blown through our windows
We spoke only of young vandals
We didn't inspect the roof or name the wind
We talked of peace and reason
Longed for lost courtesies
Sighed at the ugliness of the old world we wanted to save
Shuddered when it was said revolution controls change
And despaired when the mob that had always begged bread
Now wanted money

Only we could pay the artists and buy books
Only we had a use for quietness
See how we wrung our hands with gestures from attic friezes!
We cried with great beauty
We clung to the rags
We didn't see they made our hands dirty

And so we dug the deep dark pit
And over it spread the few yellow straws
Our slogans were tolerant! Our creed human!
We never spoke of our new masters
Or the empty streets of curfewed cities
Or neat rows of bodies outside the new annex
Each labelled at the wrist
Or the unlabelled dead who came later

THE THINKERS

In the concrete factory yard it drizzles
The stewards' mike catches the wind
Strikers with faces still oily frown as they
Strain to hear and stamp to keep warm
They ask will my opinion be heard or my question taken?
And start to bellow and wave their arms
These are signs of clear thought and judgement
To the TV screen a rabble of louts

The director doesn't open the door
It's held for him by the chauffeur
Paper and pen before each chair
Glasses and a decanter of water
Whispering in carpet-dust parches the throat
Here the workers were once sifted for profit in a giant sieve
Now the hands holding the sieve shake in fear

Hurling the workers from side to side in chaos
Things can't go on as they are
No control!
Calm voices can't hide the panic
The porter opens the door as the director leaves
On the TV screen a courteous smile on top of a white shirt
'Let's hope the men see reason'

When the men have the table and pen and ink
The view from your window will change
At one stroke you'll see many things differently
Paper and pens are the tools of reason
Who knows how to use them?
The lathe operator works to the thousandth of an inch
He's schooled in the art of discrimination
His owner demolishes houses and builds empty towers
Who knows the craft of choosing?
The lathe operator counts shillings
His owner moves millions over the board
Who knows the value of money?

The clouds didn't soak your black coat
So that it shines like the river as you run for shelter
It's the drops of rain that did it!
The icy wind didn't make the girl shake with fever
It's the little crack in the window that killed her
But round here you know nothing!
You dress the criminal in red robes instead of pulling him
    from the chair
You put his victims in thin prison overalls!
You people would let the killer come up to you with the knife
    in his hand
If he disguised himself as a surgeon!

How confused you are
It will be hard for you to think till reason wears its own
    clothes
And speaks in its own voice

ON VIOLENCE

It's said violence creates violence
Violent man is chained to a wheel
His struggles to free himself turn the wheel
Day after day he's knocked off his feet and stood on his head
There are three sounds in the world
The grinding of stone
The racing of chains over the stone
And the man's groans

If this is true the state must create revolution or war
The state is the greatest user of force
If the wheel turns the state must cause violence
It may be said the state doesn't use force in violent ways
Instead it has preachers teachers and judges
So there is no nightmare
No war dance of the devil mask with the red mouth waved on
    a stick to frighten children
No puppet of stuffed denim with helmet and gun
To kill as if it were a child playing with clay
And so the wheel stops

Consider
The scrupulous judge weighs the law in his white hand
Politely he sends a man to prison for ten years
Or he says 'Go
Take this chance to be a good worker and live by the law
I wish you well'

The last sentence is more violent than the first
It condemns the man to give his life to the judge
Teach his child the judge has a right to send its father to prison
Respect the school that made the judge
Build a wall round the judge's house to protect his loot
Hurry to work each morning to make guns for the judge to fire in the square
And be told to die in his own house or kill in his neighbour's
Or worse worse day after day to live quietly
So that the judge may give mercy that's harsher than prison

All this might be justified if in the place of violence it put order
So that the wheel stopped
It doesn't
Whatever stops man knowing himself is violent and the cause of violence
How shall a man know himself?
Let him know where he is and what he does

Consider
The man who stands in freedom on the street corner
Holds by the hand an unseen man
For twenty years this man has been mad
He is old and lies at the foot of a damp wall with his dead child in his pocket
His heart beats only to pump out his life through his wounds
He's too weak to staunch it or call for help
Who is this unseen man he holds by the hand?
Himself
If the mind had a human shape it would be this
These things were done to it by the judge who said mercy
These are the wounds of peace
The violence of freedom

More bitter than famine
Crueller than war
Deadlier than plague
It's not seen
It's hidden under the head as if that were a stone to hide truth
In such a world there is no peace
The man walks from court in freedom
The university market library broadcasting station are
    prisons
The street is the gallery of a prison
The houses on either side are cells in a prison

We're told violence is caused by violence
The argument proves the state must create revolution or war
You priests why do you pray to the god of war for peace?
You comedians why do you dance in the temple of reason?
Violence will cause violence till men know themselves
Know where they are and what they do
Know the working of judgement and mercy
Till then the strongest prison is freedom
Few try to escape from its walls
But in it we're knocked off our feet and stood on our head
As we walk in the street

TYPES OF DRAMA

The remnant theatre of the old society uses a particular sort of dénouement. There's a problem in social life. It may be lack of money or an unhappy marriage or something else. The dénouement solves the problem without changing society. A will is found or a poor man turns out to be a rich orphan. Unhappy marriages are more difficult to deal with. Though wills are rarely found the idea of finding one is easily understood. But what is 'happy ever after'? So the theme of unhappy marriage is usually avoided. Instead there's frustrated romance. If only the people could live happily together they'd live happily ever after. If they can't live together they may have to die together. The thing is to fit everyone back into a changeless society (the 'found will' and all bourgeois comedy other than some satire) or to give the social conscience a bit of a dusting (the tragedy of dying lovers).

In these plays the people on stage are themselves. In many ways they're like the audience but they're still private individuals. This doesn't seem to be true of bourgeois epic characters. King Lear and Hamlet aren't presented as themselves but in a sense as all who live.

Problems that concern everyone (not individual problems common to everyone) aren't private problems so they have no individual solutions. Lear's experience and thoughts are his own but they're also everyone else's. The resolution of his play is that although evil is virulent and the good must suffer yet they may endure. Because it's corrupted by human nature society is irredemiably evil but we're formally assured it will be better governed. This assurance isn't derived from Lear's experience and his thoughts aren't an adequate philosophy for it. Shakespeare says that Lear's suffering and partial, ineffective illumination represent the fallible condition of all human goodness. The problem is seen to be political but the solution given isn't – it recommends calmness and acceptance. Shakespeare tries to give the public problem a private solution. Lear finds his own peace and dies. This means that he finally relates to the audience in the way all other characters in bourgeois theatre relate to it. He's an individual with buttons on his jacket who resolves an epic problem – in a private way. This sort of drama was still possible when Shakespeare wrote.

Lear is a feudal king with great political power. That he gives it away doesn't affect this point – it's merely Shakespeare's device to allow him to examine the problems of goodness. Characters such as Lear contain the personal and political in one image. To him the loss of an army is personal in the way the loss of a child is to one of his soldiers. His psychology effects his political acts. If he's rash he loses battles. This means that Shakespeare can use personal imagery and the personal expression of emotion to describe political causes and events, that he can transcribe historical cause into the emotional expression of personal motives. Lear represents society in his person and mind. All members of society are members of his body and their ideas and feelings are in his head. Political determinants seem to filter through him so that he can express them as direct, subjective, human experience. That's a very powerful dramatic tool. But we have to deal with new political relationships that can't be dealt with in the same way. We can't use strikers in the way Shakespeare used kings. The defeat of a strike isn't the same sort of thing as the abdication of a king. An individual biography can't show historical movement or be a pattern for the historical understanding of society. Nor (and perhaps this has the greatest significance for drama) can individual emotions still be used to transcribe historical causes. Hamlet's poetry is put forward as the voice of history itself. But emotions only tell us how it feels to be in history not how history feels. The swimmer's feelings don't describe swimming. His feelings of determination don't tell us why he won the race. Bourgeois theatre assumes the swimmer's determination is so great that he rises out of the water and runs across it. We have to show the real mechanisms of history – the dreamtime is over. We can't use a general to encapsulate an army. A private soldier can't represent a historical pattern, as interpreted by socialism, in the way a general can represent it as it's interpreted by capitalism.

A play can show characters resolving a problem by using socialist consciousness. They may win a strike or decide to build a factory or hospital. Marriage could be looked at in the same way. These would be socialist plays to be understood and enjoyed most by socialist audiences. They're incident not propaganda plays. A propaganda play must be able to tell its message to an uninformed or resisting audience. It must stress its characters' class functions. If it's to work it may be necessary to show them as types. If the propaganda is a straightforward piece of information, such as what medicine to use, types may have a direct effect. If the information is more complex – perhaps about picketing or landlords – the audience will have to translate the types back into their own experience. Obviously general statements aren't always true about individuals. Types may draw out truths from collective experience and make them easier to see. But the audience must still compare these truths with their own experience. One woman's landlord may be better than the others. She has to understand that his 'goodness' won't provide good houses and in fact that he stops her son being educated and her daughter-in-law cured. A propaganda play may make these points too. But what it does is limited by the proper need to simplify. The audience has to develop a socialist conscious-ness able to reflect and judge from its own free will. By themselves propaganda plays can't create this consciousness. Theatre workers who don't understand this ignore some of the needs of their audience.

Both incident and propaganda plays are important parts of socialist theatre. They don't try to fit people into an unchang-ing society but to help them to change society – the only unsentimental sort of modern drama. Both may be written with wit and grave feeling. Is there another sort of socialist play, another sort of epic, in which the characters aren't only in history but are its representatives? Aren't only class types but types of history or spokespeople of its forces, so that the play embodies history itself? Such an epic wouldn't only be an account or story, it would be a poem. It would put history on stage as a dramatic reality. In it subjective qualities could again be used to transcribe history. It might help us to see and understand people in a new way.

In this form, characters, events and incidents wouldn't only be aspects of historical movement. They'd show the pattern and nature of that movement. Instead of history being filtered through an individual, reduced to him (as in King Lear), the play's figures and incidents would embody and demonstrate the total historical movement. History wouldn't be shown as immanent in an individual, individuality would be transcended by the historical pattern which it represented. Incidents would be chosen to show how historical problems arise and how they lead to resolutions. Movements spread over long periods and involving masses of people might be reflected in stories, often in simple stories. The characters wouldn't be moved by personal motives but by the forces of history. They'd be epic in analysis but not necessarily in size – after all a mouse can be the hero of an epic. The forces wouldn't be shown as abstractions. We need to show the historical abstraction but at the same time we need to show the individual characteristics – they're the means through which history works. That's really the reason why we have art – we need to show the general in the particular in order to understand ourselves. So we'd show individual quirkiness. Indeed we'd show the power of historical forces by showing the individuality, ordinariness and human vulnerability and strength of the characters who live it.

In epic theatre the individual's involvement in society is seen to be a full involvement in himself. This is possible because every life is part of history. In epic theatre dramatic development doesn't come from the individual coming to terms with himself but from his changing society so that everyone in it may be more human. This broad category includes incident and propaganda plays. And it may be that socialism needs and makes possible this other, poetic drama which impersonates history.

Perhaps the epic that was possible in the classical world will again be possible. The classical world believed (and as it was then a reasonable belief it could produce art by it) that it either understood the world or that when it didn't it understood why it didn't. In this way all was understood and accepted. Homer wrote on this assumption. All events were contained in the relationship between gods and men. The gods were knowable. Of course, to men the gods' behaviour didn't always make sense as behaviour of gods. But it made sense as behaviour of men – and gods were seen as men, different only in having superhuman powers. They didn't live in the sky but in another part of Greece. Their footprints were in the dust. Street, field, plain, quay, market, house, landscape – the home of men was the home of gods. The utensils and clothes of men were also those of gods. So accounts of daily life could describe the individual and the historical pattern at one and the same time. Christianity did away with all this. To the Greeks a god might appear anywhere. The christians didn't expect to see him. He sent a sign. Often it was the virgin – a woman who conceived without intercourse, a denial of earth, a miraculous sign-in-itself. Epic doesn't deal with signs, it is itself a sign. Christian epic wasn't possible after the Bible, and even that's said to have been written not by men but by god. In the Old Testament god makes man in his image and behaves like a man himself. But by the end of the New Testament god doesn't behave like a man anymore. He's truly mysterious. His last human act is to murder his son. After that he can't be understood. He certainly can't be understood by epic. At most he can be understood in mysticism. His power isn't superhuman but supernatural. His ways can't be explained to man. He can be known only by faith. Epic has nothing to do with faith. It's created when reason and poetry are one. That's why it should be appropriate to our age.

Socialism is a philosophy of the relationship between men

and their world. Men are the measure of all things. They may speak all things that are true. How men, society, technology and their environment relate isn't fully understood. Cause and effect aren't completely observed and explained. And some things aren't illuminated by explanation but by experience – love for example. But it's again clear what sort of explanations have meaning for us and what experiences don't need explaining. God doesn't play dice with history and men can understand how reason works in it. That's why epic is possible again.

All art aspires to the lyrical, just as truth tends to the simple. And in epic the lyric becomes objective. The artist tries to show reason in experience and appearance – and lyric is the daily appearance, the commonplace dress, of reason. It shows us the rational. It makes the epic pattern human. It's the footprint on the pathway. In the epic-lyric the individual and particular are no longer isolated but are placed in a historical, social, human pattern. That's why there's a political way of cutting bread or wearing shoes. That way is described in the epic-lyric. In it there's no conceptual division between descriptions of a battle or a meal, between a battlefield or a dinner plate – no bewilderment, no creative no-man's land. Battle, meal, field and plate are all contained in one epic-lyric form of expression. They occur in one pattern of knowable causes and recognizable appearances. Each guarantees the existence of the other, each makes the other real. The family at table, the soldiers in the field, the refugees, the children playing, all human actions, human objects and the human mind may be completely shown in the arc of one story.

ON TEXTURE

We should let the audience follow the story but we shouldn't let the story run away with the play. We should let the audience enjoy the texture.

Texture concerns what someone does, why they do it at a particular moment and how they do it. It's very like the thing we often call character. But the notion of character buries something important. It makes the source of action secret, spiritual, mysterious and in the end unknowable. It's the conjuror's white rabbit, hidden away so that at any moment it can be pulled out of the hat. But when the character is treated as part of the play's texture it's placed in its social context. Instead of being abstract and spiritual it becomes political and is seen to be a matter of class. It's no longer judged as abstract kindness, anger, pride and so on but put in a context where such abstractions can be morally judged. The ability to interpret such texture is a basic human skill although the use of the skill has to be learned. When it's learned it helps to make social living pleasant.

A young office worker takes the day off. The other office workers know he went with his girl to the country. Next day he tells them his mother was ill. He explains that she wanted him to go to work but like a good son he stayed with her. On his face: the candid expression of a good son. Perhaps it will remind his audience of their feelings for their own parents? They observe how he sits down at his desk and eagerly pulls up his chair. He works a little harder than usual. How hard is finely judged. Hard enough to show he'll make up for lost time so that extra work won't fall on others but not so hard that it shows guilt. His audience are skilled observers and they take delight in using their skill.

They even enjoy the way the boss tells them he can't increase their pay. He talks and unconsciously opens the palms of his hands to show how bare they are: nicotine stains. He is eloquent. He gestures and accidentally knocks the cigar from his desk. Stooping to get it he sympathizes with them and likens his problems to their's. The cigar rolls under the desk. He has to burrow for it. He straightens and eases the pressure of the tie on his neck. There is a slight whiff of burned carpet. After enjoying all this the office workers go on strike.

You enjoy a meal. The next day you eat the same sort of food. Between the two meals you've learned how many people suffer from malnutrition. This time you don't enjoy the food. It doesn't chew in your mouth. It chokes you. Knowledge has changed the taste. Cruelty tastes like this.

A table at the end of the room. It's beautiful, its proportions are harmonious. We can also admire the beauty and grain of wood. We know how grain is revealed by polish or wear. So we go to the table to admire the grain. It's chipped and scoured. The table was made for a ballroom or a minister's office but now it's a carpenter's workbench. We're not deceived by the elegant proportions or antique design. We look and see a workbench. We learn to know what things are by their texture. Texture is evidence of truth. Because of texture we're less easily deceived. We don't judge the office holder by his desk or uniform. We look closer to see if he has a right to office.

By understanding texture the audience admire what's good, forgive what's untrue but innocent and see through hypocrisy. It gives them insight. So don't let the story completely take over. Give the audience opportunities to use and strengthen this social skill. Think of certain moments of texture as set-pieces. Don't always astonish and surprise them but give them time to observe and consider. Reveal truth patiently, if necessary step by step. Enjoy the flow of the dialectic and the turns it makes.

We have to think rationally. Texture can't do the work of concepts. But in texture we can see and enjoy the physical appearance and working of reason.

IF WE WERE HERE

The consciousness of feudal men was limited by their primitive social world. The serf wasn't much different from the cattle he tended. He was fixed rigidly in his place by the feudal god. The renaissance made society more complex. This meant that human consciousness had to become more complex. Everyone had to take more responsibility for their social role. They either had to accept it or change it. In either case they had to reconcile their behaviour with their subjective sense of autonomy, to explain their life to themselves in the light of their sense of free will. This new subjectivity wasn't just the way a man related to himself. It was also the way he related to society and judged it and his place in it. So it had a moral aspect. It wasn't only consciousness, it was also conscience.

Shakespeare helped to create this new subjectivity. One way he did this was by using the soliloquy. In a soliloquy a character talks directly from his subjective self. He comments on the play and tells us his subjective relation to it. Imagine Hamlet without the soliloquies. The play's politics would have to be made far more feudal. Hamlet wouldn't solve his dilemma by searching his conscience. The drama would be theocratic and the solution would be what god or the Bible said it was. As it is, when Hamlet is confused and perplexed he searches for moral meaning in himself. He finds it and acts. Iago also soliloquizes. He tells us he's evil but he can't tell us why he's evil. God made him evil. Shakespeare is better on goodness than he is on evil but he's usually wrong on both. There is no evil will. The evil are banal and empty, mere functionaries of each other. Modern drama must show that the origins of good and evil are political.

Hamlet is son and heir. When he talks subjectively he talks as both. His soliloquies are both political and personal. His actions as son have subjective motives which are at the same time his objective causes as heir, politician and agent of justice. By a literary device history seems to speak its purpose directly in flesh, blood, mind and passion. Hamlet's consciousness speaks as if it were the conscience of history itself. Shakespeare doesn't have to make a distinction between subjective and objective, between motive and cause. Yet this is confusing because a motive may be mistaken but a cause cannot. When Shakespeare wrote the court had political power and the rulers were a private family as well as a state institution. This meant that Shakespeare didn't need to distinguish clearly between public and private, political and personal. He could handle the two things together so that it seemed as if political problems could have personal solutions. The state was still small, uncomplicated and mysterious enough to be described by the imagery of the human body. I Hamlet the Dane! It could even seem as if in Hamlet we felt the will and emotion of history, as if the movement of history was conveyed directly in transcriptions of human emotions, so that when Hamlet is angry history is angry and Hamlet's emotion of anger triggers a historical movement.

This made it easier for Hamlet to express a wide view, to unite individual and political morality. But now political power (or at least political weight) has passed to the mass of people. A soliloquy at court isn't the same as a soliloquy in the kitchen. The connection between personal and political can no longer be shown so simply or if it comes to that so mistakenly – because the mistake couldn't be made to seem so plausible. Hamlet is the king's son. The factory worker isn't the boss's son. His actions are collective, he isn't their sole agent. In talking from his private, subjective self the worker wouldn't describe his political world in the way Hamlet did. It's not that in Shakespeare's time anymore than in our own history moved through purely psychological drives but that people could more easily act as if it did. It seemed to

Hamlet that when he talked of himself and his family he talked of his objective political relations: the rottenness in Denmark. But when he acts he doesn't see himself, his consciousness and conscience, as a product of politics. He thinks that he dips into the great bowl of truth in his mind and takes out clean water to wash the state. When Hamlet was most private he was really most public. The Hamlet soliloquy was spoken by society and this made it politically and morally urgent. Now society can no longer be expressed politically and morally in terms of the individual and so soliloquies don't work in the same way. The individual is no longer a metaphor for the state and his private feelings can no longer be used to express cause in history or will in politics. Changes in social and political relations make a new drama urgently necessary. Poetry must also change. Until it does we can't talk rationally about ourselves. The bourgeois theatre clings to psychological drama and so it can't deal with the major dramatic themes. Hamlet's soliloquy has withered into the senile monologue of Krapp's last tape. In bourgeois drama subjectivity has replaced politics and so broken Shakespeare's joining of the two. Hamlet has nothing more to say.

Hamlet's play was called 'The Mousetrap' and ironically the detective play is the atrophied remnant of the bourgeois political play. With this in mind we can see that *Waiting for Godot* is a degenerate thriller which morally says rather less than Agatha Christie's thriller. When my play *Stone* was rehearsed I was asked who'd killed the Irishman. I said I didn't know. The answer wouldn't have helped the actors to play the play or me to write it or the audience to understand it. It would have misled all of us. The play wasn't about a murder but about its cause and all those on the unjust side of the social confrontation were guilty of it. Calling one charac- ter guilty would have been as arbitrary (as to guilt) as the conviction of a murderer is by a bourgeois court. The court isn't concerned with justice, with creating just social relations. On the contrary it wishes to maintain law and order, to strengthen the unjust social relations which are the real cause of most violence. Obviously a new drama couldn't depend on the cliff-hanging trial verdict which openly or in disguise is the essence of all remnant bourgeois drama. There the dénouement depends on individual guilt and motive is substituted for cause. Such plays can't describe our times or solve our problems. They're as irrelevant as asking why Lear gave away his power. We still have to take it from him.

The Worlds is an experimental play. It tries out various dramatic devices. It tries to find new ways to tell and prove the truth. It's not the sort of experimental play that tries to reveal the truth 'from itself', from its purely aesthetic content. There are no aesthetic answers to political problems and so none to the problems of drama. There are only political answers to aesthetics problems – which is harder to prove. It implies there's a political way to cut bread, wear shoes and see sunsets. Or rather it implies that all the ways of doing these things are political and that there's a politically right way of doing them. I've always written on the assumption that this is so and in 'Types of Drama' I have tried to show why it's so. Aesthetics are often misused. This doesn't mean that we should try to write plays without aesthetics but that we should use them properly. Human beings relate through the sensory aspect of things, through appearance, sound and so on. All communities translate knowledge and social practice into aesthetic terms. Aesthetics should be thought of as ideas translated into sensory terms and art as aesthetics with true ideas.

In *The Worlds* I tried to find contemporary equivalents for Shakespeare's soliloquy. I wanted to provide a means of informed, personal comment on the play. At the same time I wanted to show the force of history, the causes of historical change. This is the dilemma. If the working class character isn't politically conscious his subjectivity is false. It's false because his owners – his employers – and their representatives manipulate it by education, news services, welfare, law, entertainment and so on. The brain in his head isn't his but their's and so he can't talk from his subjective self objectively. His introspection wouldn't tell the truth as Hamlet's did, or at least the truth as it appeared to be to Shakespeare and his audience. The worker in this condition is riddled with subjectivity and mythology precisely because he has no objective self, no valid interpretation of objective experience. But even when the worker is objective, when he's political and understands society and his role in it, he still can't talk directly from his subjective self. He knows too much. Now what he has to say is so urgent he becomes a messenger. The Greeks – who were wise – didn't make messengers their main characters. It's clear that in time a whole new world of subjective truth will be available to socialist art. But we have to solve this problem first. You could put it in this way. Hamlet can be two-dimensional in a three-dimensional way. Of course I don't use two-dimensional pejoratively. On the contrary I use it to refer to the knowledge gained from experience and in more abstract ways, which we must have and use before we can know our real political situation, make our society more rational and develop our humanity. Often what passes in drama as profound and three-dimensional is really superficial and cheap: the individual relating only to himself. Strictly this relationship isn't possible. We still think of consciousness as reflecting itself but really self-consciousness is consciousness of the world. An individual can't be true to himself but only true to the world and whether his understanding of the world is true or false is an objective matter. Strange that 'being true to yourself' isn't usually seen as the pettiness it is when compared to being 'true to the world'. Originally it was said that the 'self' to which we were to be true was given to us by god. This vouched for its value. Now god is removed but his commandment remains: so we're left to be true to the nakedest egotism. The confusion arises in the modern mind because we still think we make our own consciousness and not that it's made by our society and what we do politically in it. Our consciousness can be compared to a machine that takes in finished products (social teachings) and either reproduces the same products or creates a new understanding of the world. What goes on in the machine – what grinds out truth and sifts knowledge – is practical experience.

If we want to show a worker as two-dimensional (or objective) then unlike Hamlet he doesn't share his subjective self with us (which Hamlet does because he's three-dimensional) but becomes a teller of slogans and theory, a bringer of the message. That's the dilemma. Without political analysis there's no socialist theatre but how can we show socialism, above all things, without showing full human beings?

The dilemma is full of opportunities. First there's a mistake to avoid. We mustn't treat personal dramas which are only a consequence of political dramas as if they were themselves full political dramas. A shop steward or lecturer sacked for being a socialist isn't dramatically interesting – politically – because he personally suffers. This would let bourgois theatre in by the side door. We need to make objective political analysis fully dramatic in its own right. This seems harsh but if we do the last properly it will include the first.

In the speech beginning 'If we were here' I've tried to push the character, for that speech, not into his Hamlet-self but say forty years ahead in time. He then talks not as he is but as he would be after we have been there. His age stays the same but he speaks with historical hindsight, with greater political consciousness and stronger political presence than he yet has. Because of this his language changes. But this is essential: the audience mustn't feel that the character has suddenly stopped being himself (he hasn't, anymore than the actor playing Hamlet stops acting when he talks directly to us) and become the spokesman of the author. What the character says must still be right for his character. His subjective individuality then helps to explain the truth of his objective, generalized statements: in the future these things will be because there are *now* people like him. So it would be nearer the truth to say that the author becomes the spokesman of his character. The actor doesn't step out of character but the audience sees the character's potential self, sees him as he could be. I call this device a public soliloquy. Perhaps Chekhov meant Vershinin to do something like this when he 'philosophizes'. But Vershinin hides in visions and expects to be laughed at. He isn't a cause of change, he stays the same and we're to accept change because of his personal faith in it. This limits his dramatic use. He doesn't speak for the author. Really he speaks against him.

Shifting time in this way isn't doing anything more awkward than Shakespeare did when he let a character 'talk-to-us-in-himself'. If it seems awkward that's because writers and audiences haven't learned to live in our time as fully and perceptively as Shakespeare and his audience knew how to live in their's. We haven't learned what's possible and necessary for us as well as they knew what was possible and necessary for them. Their drama exploited subjectivity more subtly and efficiently than ours. We should develop public soliloquy and other devices till we can use them without confusing the audience. If we understood ourselves and others more we would see people differently. Showing people in this way on stage would help our audience to create this understanding. They could delight in these new devices and see their own strength in them.

The quality of public soliloquy, of a commentary which the character has the right to speak (and which the actor and the writer have won for him) needn't be confined to moments in a play. A large part, perhaps all, of Scene Four (Part One) of *The Worlds* could be acted as a group public soliloquy. Whole characters or groups could be permeated with public soliloquy so that we feel they're both in and outside their time and aren't eternal prisoners of the present appearance of things. Such a play wouldn't just record events but would be a sustained public soliloquy, a politically informed commentary on what the play records. Otherwise how can socialist writers put three-dimensional characters on stage? We risk showing characters merely as schematized class functions or as still being essentially bourgeois. That's no better than showing them as bluff jokers who try to slip in a message when no one's looking. Unfortunately that's also when no one's thinking.

Actors must act lives not abstractions. Otherwise one of the main strengths of drama is wasted. Class functions must be shown or the drama is meaningless but we need to extend our ways of showing them. We must show that politically conscious figures are full human beings, that their class function is a complete self function and that in consciously being members of their class they're also fully themselves. Socialist art has nothing to do with the arbitrary, fanciful rigmarole of bourgois art but neither is it a restriction. It is in the way the truth is told and that makes it synonymous with freedom. Our audience is new, it is not the audience of the earlier socialist theatre. The continuing industrial revolution and comparative affluence have satisfied some of their needs, hidden others and given new ones. They behave and see the world differently. We have to deal not merely with the crimes of capitalism but with its excuses, evasions and superficial successes. As capitalism becomes cruder it becomes more sophisticated – and the working class more subtle and clear-sighted. Drama must deal with the world as it is. It must find its use. When society changes it mustn't repeat itself. Capitalism has a need for nostalgia because the quality of its culture and intellectual life deteriorates no matter what goods it provides. But we have no need to look to the past in this way. We should create a new culture.

Tackling the dilemma in this and other ways would let us create real sensitivity and subjective discrimination. These qualities are necessary to human society. Sensitivity is still associated with Bloomsbury but that sort of sensitivity is false, cut off from knowledge of the real world by an escape into a dark, fragile, ghostly world of eccentrics. It sees political relations and the use of power as always barbarous. Well, since it discards social and political obligations in this way it has no moral aspect. It merely feeds on aesthetics, which by itself is a poison. The subjective self becomes sensitive and discriminating only when it's shaped by objective knowledge, when knowledge and experience of the real world illuminate and reform subjective individuality. It's a form taken by reason and morals, the individual's way of possessing the truth. In the past sensitivity was often pale and fanciful because it belonged to a culture which instead of revealing the world concealed it. But we cannot be human without moral, discriminating sensitivity. It expresses understanding of history, society and the world in subjective terms. How can we be rational and human without that?

The renaissance developed subjectivity but at the same time prostituted it to the objectivity of the business ethic. This was reflected in subjectivity in the haunted puritan conscience and the witch-hunt. Its modern counterpart is fascist racism. Socialism could resolve most of the antagonisms between objectivity and subjectivity. It would let us live in the world as it is and so be our true selves, instead of living in the world as it is run for the benefit of a few – with all the mythology, injustice and distortions in consciousness and conscience that follow. All this was historically necessary and it had the justification that for a time it created order. Now it creates disorder. Feudalism saw workers as purely objective: as little more than beasts, and the church said beasts had no souls. And even what little subjectivity workers did have wasn't owned by them, it was owned by god. Capitalism sees workers as machines and all that goes into them as raw materials. It sees a holiday on the Costa Brava or a colour TV set as raw materials for making cars or cans. No doubt many who tell us socialism and technology will turn us into robots would like us to be beasts or machines. But socialism could create an objective sensitivity and so make us fully human.

A character strengthened with two-dimensional political analysis has three-dimensional wholeness. He has a rational, moral psychology with which he understands the world as well as himself and is able to develop humanely in step with changing technology. His humanity and sensitivity are strengths. He is whole, not the rump Hamlet of late bourgeois theatre, the Krapp with nothing to say. His public soliloquy is spoken for himself and for others too. In this paragraph I've dropped the distinction between characters in the play and in the audience. Culture is our means of understanding and saying what we are and ought to be. This image, with the appropriate mind and conduct, changes historically. Theatre workers are part of the audience, at most no more than its spokesmen. We can say that the audience is ready to create a new image and a new culture.

THE ART OF THE AUDIENCE

Eagerly the dumb hear the singer
And the crippled still run the race
So strong do men struggle
But actors are only shadows
The stage is an image of the world where the audience act
We move with their gestures
We speak language they have refined.
We mourn because they mourn and we study their mourning
We have wit because they laugh

We wear their clothes
The fire doesn't set light to itself.
There's no foreign land called art
Art doesn't create its own truth
Our blood is paste
We die and return with the living

Scrupulously we enter their struggle
To show the clash of classes
To speak precisely the concepts to be drawn
From their experience
To sharpen the sharp mind
To show iron freedom
To show that at the horizon where light enters the world
A world is still hidden

What is art?
It puts the incident into the concept
The stone into the mosaic
It fits each word to the epic
We march over continents in a small room
In two hours we pass through centuries
And show how every hour leads to the next
And the years that wait in a day
We show how a soldier stands in a corner of every kitchen
Like a sentry over a pass
We study the waves
They remind us of the worker's creased brow

Our form: clarity order precision
Our tools: colour action sound
Our weapons: anger laughter judgement
Our face is a mirror that shows the spectator his face
In us he studies himself and his friends
He learns to know himself and to fight the exploiter

We wish to show how the crisis leads to the solution
How shall the audience judge what we show?
Art is more than the intellectual knowledge of truth
It's social
The audience ask will this solve the crisis played on our
    streets?
If our solution is wrong we've pretended their houses are
    painted flats
But they built the houses
Carrying bricks and pouring concrete
And the knowledge of how the world works
Gained by carrying and pouring
Is the knowledge by which truth is judged
In art and everything else

Who are our audience?
We write for those who carry bricks
Not those who hire builders
The hirer's world is a dream that floats on painted clouds
We speak to him if he sits in our audience
But he's an onlooker
Only the others can judge
Only they have the knowledge to judge
The hirer reverses all human values
We write for those he exploits
If we give them a key they know if it will open the door
They made the door
It's as simple as that
If our theatre shows beauty wisdom and skill
It's because our audience know how these things should be
    used

So we show the audience its great talents
We study the art of the audience

A POEM

In things there is order
Stone is hard
Water is liquid
We drink water
When we don't drink we die
When we drink poison we die
Little grows in sand

There's order too in human affairs
Not so simple as the order of stone and water
Harder to see but with laws as strong
They're part of the order of all things
Part of the iron law
Stones water men and all things are in iron law

The tree has roots
Through them it takes water
We don't take what we need in so simple a way
We take what we need through society
It's as if the tree fetched water to its roots

The tree doesn't think how to take water
Or imagine it's stone
The tree doesn't move
Roots are the way it's in the world
Men move and make new ways to be in the world
Plough
      Sledge
            Tractor
               Plane
                     are ways to be in the world
They are ways as roots are a way

Stones trees and dogs evolve through eons
Such creatures and things change as their place changes
Evolution makes mountains trees and dogs
It's slow
Trees rarely change their way
The way of the dog rarely changes till we change it
In the way of man there is great change
When our way changes we change
We change our way
We change the place where we are
We change it quickly
We must change as quickly as we change the place where we
    are
We don't change in eons we change in history
What wonder the change we bring to the world!
We make history and so make ourselves
We change quickly but still in the iron law
The means by which a thing is in the world is its way
Trees may not move from their place
Fish may not fly
And men must follow the way of men

If trees lost their roots they wouldn't be trees
When the ground's parched the roots are dry and the tree
    withers
We change the place where we are
We change the means by which we live
We change what we are
We change our place quickly
It's not enough if our feet change as feet change in eons
Feet can't change quickly enough
We change our mind
The mind changes quickly
We must change quickly
History is fast

We imagine
We couldn't think unless we imagined
We couldn't work unless we imagined
We couldn't make a machine unless we imagined
We couldn't make a poem unless we imagined
We can't know everything
There's no time to see round corners
We need imagination to understand what's real
We need imagination to live in history
If we didn't imagine we'd be as slow and cumbersome as
  wooden puppets
We'd be in eons
We may imagine the real to be false
With a new strength a new weakness

Imagination helps us to learn
It makes thinking more skillful
Imagination is iron law yet free to be false
We imagine we're wise
We imagine blackmen or whitemen are devils
Trees and stones can't imagine
They're in the world of iron law
It's also in iron law that to live in history we must imagine
In imagination there's freedom and slavery
Imagination to men is as the pole star to the sailor or the axe to
  the tree
On us lie the burdens of morals and choice
These like roots are a way to be in the world
Without them we'd be in eons

Roots and leaves are the tree's way to be in the world
By these means it makes part of the world into itself
All our abilities are means in this way
They're iron law

We're free yet in iron law
We imagine and think
These are means by which we're part of the world and make
    part of the world us
They're the way we're in the world

History is the way we're in the world
Society is the way we're in history
Society organizes us into a way to be in the world
So we eat drink and build
This is a means as roots are means
Society organizes us to live together and make tools
We prosper and win great power and learning
Those who can be taught can be told
We're told what we are
But we are what we do because that's the means by which we
    are
We're told but we also learn by ourself
Society tells us what we are in society
The branch doesn't tell the leaf to be part of the tree
We're not as safe as the tree from the axe

We're born in ignorance
We're born to question
That's why we're men
When the tree first grows it's already a tree
We're not men when we start to live
We don't know what we are till we learn
We learn to be men
To be human or inhuman
The tree can't learn to be stone
We must be born in ignorance or our minds would be as rigid
    as stone
We change the world
As the world changes our mind changes

We are free to change
We must be free to learn

What a thing is depends on what it gets and how it gets it
The tree takes water through roots
We take our share of the world through work
We're masters servants workers and children
All men breathe and sleep in one way
They're not all in the world in one way
They're master or servant
They're in the world in two ways

We're in society
Society tells us our place in society
Society tells us what we are
Society calls us master or servant
Society tells us that's also our name in the world
We are the way we're in the world
The world can't lie
Trees are trees
Men are in the world only as the men they are
Society can lie
Men are in society and society is in the world
Men are not in society in the same way they're in the world
We change the world and this changes what we are
What we are in society changes
Society may not accept this change
But if society lies it's still in the world
All things in the world are in iron law
Iron law is the way all things are in the world
Men are society's way of being in the world
As men change their world they change themselves
Society doesn't change as quickly as men change
Men must change society because that's the way they're in
    the world

Wind and fire make things in eons
Society teaches us and makes us
We have two conducts and two minds
What we are in the world and what we are in society
Men must be in society in the way they're in the world or
    there's chaos
We must change society to complete the change in ourself
As we change society we must change ourself but society tells
    us who we are
It's as if the roots could tell the tree to fly
We may not be what society tells us we are
How shall we judge?

Society is the way the world's farmed and mined
It's the way we share what we take and make
It places us in its organisation
Earth doesn't own the tree or the tree the earth
The means by which it takes water isn't owned
No owner tells the tree what it is
What a tree is isn't owned
Society owns the earth
Society owns the means by which we live
Society owns the way we're in the world
Society owns men
Society owns the image of man
Society tells each man what he is and what all other men are
Society owns
Society is owned

To farm mine and fish there must be order
Society is order
Without order we can't farm mine and fish
There's chaos
As much as if the water turned to stone and the tree withered

Men live together
Men must work together

Some men know they lie
Others lie but don't know it
Men who imagine are free to imagine the false
Here are two lies

   1.
   This world isn't real
   The real world is in eons
   Our conduct in the unreal world decides what we do in
      eons
   2.

   The tree is still
   Men move and cast stones at each other
   We're animals
   Society is the way we stop tearing out our neighbour's
      throat
   Those who own society stop us tearing out our neighbour's
      throat
   The owners are strong with the wisdom of sages

If goodness is weak and must be protected by society then
   society is more evil than those who're in it
If goodness is weak it can't get power and so society is ruled
   by the evil and strong
If men are animals society must be more corrupt than the
   animals in it
If we're good and wise enough to create societies we're good
   and wise enough to live without them
If goodness and wisdom weren't stronger than ignorance and
   evil we wouldn't have created societies
Instead of society there could be friendship

All that's in history changes
The society slow to change when men change is soon corrupt
Reason works quickly or slowly
Gradually or in crisis

The tree isn't taught to be a tree
Society teaches us the conduct of men
We farm and mine and make and conduct ourselves in the
 ways to do this
Otherwise we couldn't do what we do
We're free to imagine but we're not free to imagine we don't
 do what we do
We have the mind of the people who do it
Society can't give us the mind of those who don't do it
Anymore than roots can tell trees to fly
Our way to be in the world is to have the mind to do what we
 do
We make our mind by what we do
Our mind makes us what we are
We learn what we are from what we do
We're what we do and this is our way to be in the
 world
But society teaches us what we are in society
It teaches us that what we are in society is also what we are in
 the world
It tells us our social position is given to us by nature
That would be reasonable if we were in society what we are in
 the world
Then reason and nature would be one
But society stands between us and the world
It may teach us falsely
It may deny what we learn by what we do in the world
Teaching may conflict with experience
Teaching may conflict with the conduct we need in order to
 live in society as we are in the world

If trees were in society society would often tell them to fly and
    punish them for not flying
When we change we must change society
The mind enshrined or encrusted in social institutions may
    be the mind of men who lived long ago

Trees and stones are hard
We struggle to change them
Hardness resists change
Society is hard
Society is owned by the past
By the dead bones who own flesh
Society tells men how to live
But they also learn how to live from what they do
They learn from experience
From working together
Men change when they learn new ways of working
Society has schools churches and courts to tell us what we are
Social institutions are the means by which we're in the world
They're also the means by which society is owned
Owners of society own its institutions
They own the image of man – of what man ought to be
Owners of society don't own men's experience

Society must be in the world in the way men are in the world
    or men have two minds and two conducts
Then it seems to them they're in two worlds
But the world is real and we're what we do in the real world
Society has pilots and tractor drivers
Society has the minds and conduct of pilots and tractor
    drivers
That's the way society is in the world
Pilots and tractor drivers are made by what they do
Society is owned by the past but needs pilots and tractor
    drivers

Society owned by the past teaches tractor drivers they're
    ploughmen and pilots they're waggoners
Society owned by the past puts men into society in a false
    way
When men are in society in the way they're in the world
    society is rational
Their minds and conduct are rational
And they live in reason
When men are not in society in the way they're in the world
    society is irrational
And their minds and conduct are either irrational – dictated
    to them by society
Or rational – formed by what they do in the world and their
    struggle to change society

Irrational men can't co-operate
Their society is organised by force and myth
Force and myth can't make irrational society stable
Irrational society deteriorates
A pilot with a waggoner's mind can fly – even a charioteer
    could drive a tank
But a pilot can't be human in a waggoner's society
In a waggoner's society a pilot understands planes but
    nothing of men
His society isn't human and he isn't human
Men with two minds and two conducts aren't human
They can't treat themselves or other men as human
They become human only when they struggle to make society
    rational
Men with two minds and two conducts can't know them-
    selves or other men
They're irrational
Irrational men fear and panic
Men who fear and panic believe what they imagine
Men act on what they believe

The society of pilot-waggoners and ploughmen-tractor
    drivers falls
It says men behave badly because they're animals
It's easier to justify force when it's used against animals than
    when it's used against men
Irrational society uses fear fraud and force against men
    because it thinks they're animals
There is chaos!

Courts universities and other social institutions often repress
    the needs of those who work in factories power stations and
    other modern institutions
All irrational social institutions conflict with human practice
This is the dilemma
Society must control men so that they can live and work in the
    world together
Men must control society so that they can live in society in a
    human way
Otherwise society is inhuman and men are inhuman
Social institutions don't change as men change
Men change as they change the world
Men can't resist this change – they change because of what
    they do
Society resists change
Society is owned
All changes in society change the ownership of society
Societies that can't change in peace change by force
Iron law

The tree bends in storm
We make the storm that bends us
So strange are we!
As if we created the elements in ourselves
Jove-like we hurl the thunder bolt
Scamander flooded the plains of Troy

We flood history
Men become their own chaos because they're their own
   creators
There's danger in freedom
But freedom is iron law

Iron law
When men are in two minds and with two conducts society is
   torn apart
We who live in history are free to fall into chaos
We're not free to fall out of history
We fall into chaos when we're false to what we are
We are what we do in the world
When we don't follow the iron law it judges us harshly
But men will have reason – what they do in the world
   demands it
If history is about to turn back men take to the streets and
   bring her home
Once men are in history they can't be animals
Those who own society seek unreason
Their hirelings teach it and their soldiers kill in its name
But reason comes to the world because men work
We work and change the world and change ourselves
That's the way we're in the world
Let us talk of these men of change
Men who change the world and themselves so that they're
   also the men who change their society
Men who change society so that it's in the world in the way
   they're in the world are the seekers of reason
They seek reason in society because of the way they're in the
   world
They can't be in the world without seeking reason
Men can't pull back from being men
The horses of history can't shy in the shafts or men jump
   from her cart

Men must know who they are
That's the way they're in the world

Society organizes us to farm mine and fish
Men change when the way they work changes
Then the dealings between men change
Society doesn't change as we change
Society does nothing to the world
Society does things to the minds of men
Yet it's as if it were a tree that grew from men's brains
Of trees we say this: when the soil changes the tree changes
Society teaches and organizes men to do things in the world
Society has no way of changing
Society can only make men in its image of men
Men must make society in their image
When men change as what they do in the world changes they
    change society so that they can have one mind and one
    conduct
Men change their society or the farming fishing and mining
    go badly
The tools are misused
And men can't live in co-operation with one another
They are inhuman
They will not take responsibility for their society
Society is full of panic and fear and violence

Men change but the world doesn't tell them they're changed
The world tells nothing
Men are the way the world says what it is
The world is the place of trees and stones
Men know they change but not what they've become
They see and think in new ways
Society doesn't teach them how they've changed
It gives the child's book to the man
There is chaos

Men must speak the truth to one another
Talk together so that they understand one another
When they know what they are they're human
When they don't know what they are they're inhuman
If they're taught myths there's chaos
If they believe myths the axe is brought to the tree
If they're taught truth then experience and teaching are one
The machines and tools are well used
All men are human
The image of man is human
And men treat each other as friend

Grain isn't taken straight from the field to the table
Coal isn't taken straight from the mine to the furnace
Cotton is woven before it's worn
All that a man uses passes through the hands of all other men
Bread passes through courts universities and prisons before
    it's eaten
Yes it passes through the empty mouths of the starving before
    you eat it
That jacket's handled by kings beggars teachers children and
    madmen
It's covered bodies and mothers have wept beside it before
    you wore it
What's in a room is also in a city
The way it's owned depends on who owns the city
We own wear eat and learn prisons courts hospitals schools
Do I take food from a beggar?
Do I take my coat from the poor?
Do I learn wisdom from a madman?
Is my house a resting place for the dead?
I have two conducts: I steal the coat and wear it as if it were
    not stolen
Yes I wear his coat when I send him to prison!
When I strip am I covered in stolen flesh?

Write down on this all that I say said the doctor of law as he
tore a strip from his dunce's cap and handed it to his
student

Iron law
We eat lies or truths
We wear lies or truths
We teach lies or truths
We walk in lies or truths
One or the other
If we're in society in a false way we're the tree growing on
rock
Owls fly from her branches they do not trust her
The fox will not house her cubs under her roots
The mole will not dig in her shadow
What's irrational offends the elements in man
There's chaos

History is the struggle for reason
Without reason we fall into chaos and suffer in chaos
So we seek reason
It's the way we're in the world
There's no other way men can be in the world
Men who don't seek reason seek the irrational
Such men destroy themselves
The owners of men don't seek reason
That have weapons to destroy us
The greater the weapon the faster history runs

Iron law
We can't be destroyed because the animal in us overtakes us
History outran the beasts long ago
We can't be destroyed by what comes from the past
We make the future
Make it irrationally and it will destroy you

History can't forget
Destroy the tractors and planes – you're still the men who made them!
They made you
Understand what you are
Men who don't seek understanding destroy society
Unless we seek understanding society is barbarous
Men revolt against barbarity
Men struggle to be what they do
Men struggle to be what they are
Men struggle to learn what they are
Men struggle to be human
We long to live in a society which tells us what we are
Our struggles to change society are our struggles to be ourself
The old society stops us being human
Men are what they do but they must learn what they are
The mind needs schooling in concepts
We need reason in social institutions so that society may live in accord
We need society in which human gestures have meaning
An action must mean the same in society as it means in the world
Yet it's still not so!
They throw bones to the beggars
Men's bones? Who can tell in this place?
If I'm kind will those who torment the poor sleep sounder at night?
What men do has two aspects
An action is done in society and in the world
Men can't be human in an irrational society
They revolt against unreason
The seeking of reason is the seeking of justice
Wherever men are there is the shout for justice
The call for reason

Men can't stop their struggle for reason till they have it or are
   wiped from the face of the earth
Men don't seek justice because some of them are born just or
   with this strange desire
Men don't seek justice because their souls seek it
Men seek justice because that's the way they're in the world
Justice is making the two worlds one
We can't be in the world in another way
We can't be water or stone
We're in the world in the order of the world
In iron law
The iron law is that men seek justice and reason
We seek it because we change the place where we are and so
   change ourselves so that we must change our society
We seek it because the stone is hard and the tree's branches
   shake in wind
We seek it because of what we do
We seek it because we eat sleep dress build love and
   work
Our hands as they till the earth and tend machines gesture for
   justice
When the two minds and two conducts are one there'll be
   reason and justice
A good act will be good in both worlds
Not good in one and evil in another
If I feed the beggar at the wayside the prince will not sleep
   sounder in his tower
It is down
Evil will be the same in both worlds
And men won't be torn apart
The judge will be just

Iron law
There must be this order because of the way we're in the
   world

The tool which makes change
The tool-user's mind and conduct
The society which teaches him to use tools and live together
    with other men
Must relate together in reason
Then society will be the home and guardian of friends
The elements in man be at peace
And the image of man be human

The search for reason shapes history
The sleeper struggles to find comfort
He calls in his sleep
History is the human day and already the sleeper wakes
He will not struggle in dreams but walk the earth
He will talk reason to friends
Two minds and two conducts will be one
We will know the world we're in
And what we are

Tools change the world and the tool-user
Only the tool-user knows how to use tools
Only he knows the tool-user
Only he knows what men are
Only he knows what society ought to be
The tapping of tools are the seconds of history
We struggle to make society a tool to make men who live and
    change in peace
So that man is the image of man

Then the ploughman won't be flogged to the tractor
The tractor driver will sit in the tractor and plough over
    common fields
Not rake the rubble of Lidice
Schools will teach truth written before men could read and
    truth men have written

Reason will not go in prison uniform or the scientist in fool's
    motley
The boats will put out to sea and cast nets for fish
And the world will be run by the fishers of fish
Not by those who cast nets to fish in the sea for statues of
    stone

ON AESTHETICS

The trees at Auschwitz were beautiful but did the guards and
prisoners see the same beauty?

Prisoners painted pictures of camp life. Their pictures
showed what that life was like. They're images of the truth.
They're beautiful. Could an overseer have painted the same
pictures? No, we paint what we see. The overseer couldn't
have seen what life was like in the camp. He'd paint an image
of a lie. It would be irrational. I don't know of such a painting
but imagine how it would show a guard.

Some prisoners were killed for painting pictures. Were
they killed because of what they painted or how they painted
it? The paintings were beautiful because the painters wanted
to record the truth and had the skill to do so. The overseer
wasn't interested in truth and so couldn't see its beauty. It
would be impossible for him to say 'This hanging shouldn't
have been painted. All the same the painting has great beauty
and must be shown to all who love beauty.'

Aesthetic judgements aren't based on the abstract appearance of things but on what we know or think we know about
them. Aesthetic appearance changes as knowledge changes.
If our understanding of the world is rational we can discrimi-
nate between beauty and ugliness. If it's irrational we can't
make this discrimination clearly.

The tree is beautiful. It grew at Auschwitz and this makes
it more beautiful to those who see the world rationally. To

them a tree is more beautiful because it grows anywhere in the world in which there is Auschwitz. It's more beautiful because they understand why Auschwitz was built and can use their understanding to defeat its builders.

If men and all other creatures were immortal and all things immutable then men wouldn't find anything beautiful. We have a sense of beauty because we're mortal. The sense comes from knowledge of change. All beauty reminds us that we're human. But the sense of beauty is political and not metaphysical. It doesn't come from the banal confrontation of life and death. If it did beauty would always be sad. As it is, it's always joyful. This is because the confrontation is between cruelty, stupidity and waste and reason, love and humanity. Between death and life that's decent, moral, human and sane. This sort of life is created by reason working in history. It means that beauty is politically determined. Some things are more beautiful than others. But to the rational all things in nature are beautiful and most other things are beautiful as well.

Beauty isn't what we see or sense in another way but depends on our relation to what we see or sense in another way, on what we know or think we know about it. Aesthetics isn't about abstract seeing but our human relation to things. We can't be taught to see abstract beauty. We can be taught what stops us seeing beauty or makes us see it as ugliness. How clearly we see depends on how well we understand.

All ugliness is made by men. Only they are able to see ugliness, desire it and bring it into the world. They often call it beauty. When men assemble or disassemble things they may make them less beautiful. Ugliness is the image of the irrational. The irrational see beauty as ugliness and ugliness as beauty. But the ugliness which they see as beauty doesn't appear as real beauty even to them: it's clouded, phantom-like, a dream. The irrational can't see real beauty. All that the irrational see as real is ugliness. That's why destruction attracts them. The rational see that all things not made ugly by men are beautiful. Men may themselves be ugly. The face of the SS overseer is ugly. He and others have made it ugly.

Men may make things more beautiful. Rembrandt makes a painting by arranging natural aesthetic elements (such as colours and shapes, the abstracts used in representation) and images or parts of images of things that are partly natural and partly made by men and their society (such as clothes or the human face with its images of nature, biography and history). Artists arrange images and natural qualities into new forms. When they create art they don't use aesthetic qualities in an arbitrary way. Riding a bicycle over a wet canvas creates beauty when it's confronted (in the mind) with the decadent arbitrariness of the disciplined, dead photographic realism of the academic portrait.

A work of art is seen politically. Aesthetic elements, considered apart from images, are also seen politically. Art adds comment to aesthetic elements. This increases our enjoyment of them. Good form is produced by the working of reason in history and by the understanding of this working. We see things historically. This is true of whatever we reproduce in art: scenes, still lives, portraits, abstracts and so on. The way men recreate natural qualities and images into works of art (or see works of art) is the same as the way they see the real world. What creates excellence in art? Seeing rationally. That is, to see the world as it is, or rather as real as it can rationally be understood and therefore seen at the time. As men increase their understanding of their relationship to the world so the appearance of the world changes. As time passes it's possible for more people to understand the art of the past because in some ways it becomes easier to understand. Often understanding is first achieved through struggle and effort. To portray the world more rationally the artist must also struggle. Human knowledge and experience, and the creative work of the artist, elucidate and strengthen each other. An artist shows the rational appearance of things at a particular time. He records historically. If rational art shows the reality of the appearance of things it follows that it can also show the reality in and by which they change – that is, it can show the force of history itself revealed in the present. When he does this the artist shows the lasting strength of human reason. He also shows our reason for living, since we're the expressors of the force of history. This is the most creative form of art. The pot doesn't show the marks of the potter's hands or his wheel. The form is created by the two forces working on the clay. From the pot we read the strength of the elemental forces that make it. The image of the force of history should be thought of as appearing in works of art in the same way.

The world is a place of natural aesthetic qualities. Socialism is produced by being in the world in a creative way. Socialist consciousness sees the world differently from other forms of consciousness. It sees it to be more beautiful than it is as seen by earlier forms of consciousness that survive but have out-lived their creative period. When these earlier forms were created they would (provided they were the rational forms of their time) have seen the world to be more beautiful than it was as seen by still earlier forms. In our time the confrontation in our species between reason and irrationalism – a confrontation made necessary by the biological and physical nature of things – is between socialism and fascism. Of course not all prisoners in fascist concentration camps are socialists. But all enemies of fascism see more rationally (and so distinguish more accurately between beauty and ugliness) than its supporters. However not all who fight fascism are its rational enemies. Some, such as English tories, are merely its political opponents. They can't create rational art and indeed most of them insist on the practical irrelevance or even the nihilism of art. A humane artist who isn't a socialist may make images that contain the ideal in an abstract way. They are dream images, phantasmagoria. But rational art is practical. The final, ideal appearance of reason will be created by the struggle for reason. Only artists involved in this struggle can see and paint (according to their skill) the reality of its image in the present. They see the ideal as practical and man-made, not as a visionary dream. Abstract idealized images lack the moral authority of rational art. They're not proved to be art by the practicality of reason in them. In them the ideal is static.

We see objective things subjectively. Different men see the same painting differently. Not all men see the same Giotto scene. The artist sees a chair in one way. X may see the chair differently. The artist and X may see the artist's painting of the chair differently. Those with a rational consciousness see things as they really are, or rather as they really are for their time. They will really be different for later times. Beauty has a historical form. Shakespeare didn't have to wonder if an aeroplane is beautiful. He saw *his* world in a rational way and recorded what was seen by the rational mind of his time. Because he did this with skill he created beauty. Rational men can see the historical appearance of reason in earlier art but irrational men can't. That's why the academic understanding of Shakespeare usually trivializes him. Seeing things as they really are is like seeing them in a practical way. Beauty and ugliness are real when they're seen rationally. When it's seen irrationally beauty is dream-like and phantasmagoric. When the irrational see ugliness it has the quality of nightmare of which the dreamer is in charge. All societies and all people live in one calendar time but many live in many cultural times. Hitler is a medieval man seeing an aeroplane. He sees a vision, it might be a god. It doesn't have the reality which belongs to beauty. This means that Hitler can't understand the world in which the aeroplane flies. He sees the world irrationally, that is destructively. Reactionary artists create reactionary images, dream-images that obscure the truth. They are like a screen of dreams wrapped round a reactionary's head.

An artist can help us to see more clearly. He's in a special rational, moral relation to what he records. But a work of art doesn't reveal truth to everyone who looks at it. The SS man sees what the artist records and may even recognize some of its truth. The enemy in the dock may be beautiful just as the innocent may be sinister. But the SS man sees the picture as tainted, as beautiful *and* ugly. It repels or fascinates him. He wants to destroy it or is obsessed by it in another way. These aren't his subjective reactions to a common appearance shared by him and the artist. His mind distorts what it sees. He doesn't see the objective beauty created by the artist because he can't judge it rationally and morally. The beauty the artist creates is an image of the rational understanding appropriate to the time it's created. It combines moral imperatives with political imperatives rationally appropriate to that particular stage in human development. The consciousness of the SS man doesn't belong to the present. His head is here but what's in it is in the past. His cultural time isn't his calendar time. When he paints the picture is being painted hundreds of years ago.

Intellectual discourse is rarely poetry. But conversation on factory floors and in bread shops is a form of poetry. In these places people relate ideas to words and their voice to each other's in a poetical way. If people didn't normally speak poetry they'd sound odd. One aim of culture is to change the concepts in colloquial speech so that people aren't mystified and made to despair by the irrational appearance of the world. But even in a mystified world ordinary people must usually speak poetry in order to survive, to be accepted in ordinary social relations. This is because ordinary people are ordinarily practical and this places them close to one element in reason. It's only in a wholly irrational world (SS soldiers in their barracks for example) that they stop speaking poetry and speak melodramatically instead. Formal poetry is only more beautiful than bread-shop conversation when its concepts are more rational. Often out of sheer practical necessity the concepts used on the shop-floor are more practical than those used in a university. A machine either does what it's made to do or it doesn't. This produces a practicality in its makers and users (not necessarily in its sellers, of course) that can extend to the rest of their consciousness. A university doesn't produce a machine, it produces a mind. A mind that doesn't know reality can invent a false one. Probably most literature teachers find more poetry in their mortgage than in Shakespeare. They understand their mortgage better and it means more to them and so they can interpret it practically. If this wasn't so universities would be very different.

An SS man and a socialist see the same sunset differently. Seeing depends on the seers objectivity: how objective is his subjectivity? This depends on his culture and this depends on his class and political position. We see what we know or think we know. We don't see a Rembrandt portrait of a jew as Hitler saw it. We don't see the tree at Auschwitz as Himmler saw it. If the biological act of seeing had a built in moral discrimination then the SS and the socialist would see the same aesthetic qualities, the same beauty, in the same things. Things would appear the same to them. If they did seeing would be a very privileged activity – all other forms of moral judgement may be mistaken. It can hardly be denied that our moral apprehension of something changes the way it appears to us. I think our moral state (which depends on our rational state) changes the appearance of all things to us. We think that the way we see is analagous to the way we feel. Usually if we put our hands into a bowl of hot water all of us who do so feel the heat. But not if some of us have first put our hands in ice. Cultures can act like the ice. We see through our culture and so we see through extremes. Men see sunsets differently just as they see prisoners in the dock differently. If Hitler saw the Rembrandt portrait of a jew as we see it he wouldn't have been a racist who killed jews. If Hitler saw the Rembrandt portrait of a white arian gentile as we see it he wouldn't have been a racist who gassed jews. If Hitler saw the sunset as we see it he wouldn't have been a racist who gassed jews. We can't put ourself into a state of moral and political neutrality when we look at the world or a painting of it. All seeing is like an identity parade. We look for the truth. Only those who help to make the truth can know it and recognize it. Truth, morality and the appearance of things are politically determined.

The tree is there for everyone to see but we create what we see. We see subjectively. Usually we broadly agree about what we see. The SS man and the socialist see a teacup. The different ways of seeing the teacup aren't a problem because they usually have little practical consequence. Differences are usually noticed only when they have a marked practical consequence. Most of us see the red traffic light in the same way. Or at least we see it as a traffic light in the same way – not for example as part of our reflections while we wait at the crossing. We see the red traffic light and stop. We don't all see red flag in the same way. The response to this isn't as simple and uniform as stopping at the red traffic light. The question is, do we see the sunset in the way we see the red flag or the way we see the red traffic light? When we see the red traffic light we're in a car. When we see the sunset we're in our life, we're aware of the world and the men in it. Clearly this is also the way in which we see the red flag. Finally of course that's also the way we're aware in the car, because the car's in the world. So there's a political way of seeing and doing everything. But aesthetic appearances don't call out in us a conventional and conditioned response in the way the red traffic light largely does. They call out our whole life. The SS man can't see the tree as beautiful because he sees it in the way the motorist sees the traffic light. But a man may see the tree to which he's taken to be hanged as beautiful.

People might disagree if you told them their neighbour sees the sunset differently from the way they see it, that in effect he sees a different sunset. They're less likely to disagree if you said that Rembrandt saw a different sunset. This is because Rembrandt is thought to have been more creative than ordinary people. In fact he wasn't. Creativity is seeing the world rationally, that's all. Rembrandt saw more rationally than some but not all people in his time. He was exceptional not in creativity but in skill. His skill allowed him to record what he saw. Seeing a picture involves as much creativity as painting it. Fortunately creativity is very common. It would be even more common if society didn't so often try to repress it. Most people can be as creative as Rembrandt. If they weren't we couldn't live in human societies. The same creativity can be used (depending on the skill) to paint, compose music, run a home, teach, change society, care for others, live a decent life and so on. All these activities may call out the whole of our life.

ON PROBLEMS

The creator needs problems
The problem is an unlearned skill
In solving problems the creator learns skills
He uses skills to make new skills
Out of problems

The worker has only problems and skills
Respect the problem!
Don't turn back or aside when you see it
Go to it
It holds the secret of change

Look at the problem closely
Understand it has many sides
But few solutions
Before the solutions are known
You must know the sides

This is the law of nature
The chain snaps at the weakest point
Follow the same law
To release the prisoner
Search the chain for the weakest point
Then aim the axe

At each new step in the race
The runner places his foot
On the edge of his reach
Each step touches this boundary
How else can he win the race?

Sun ripens or scorches
Frost may kill the young shoots
Wind scatter the sheaves
Drought turn fertile earth to dust
Or rain mire it
These are the farmer's problems
When he knows his problems the harvest is safer
He studies the earth and the sky
Or plants in the wrong season

A storm may sink the ship
Or a hurricane sweep the sailor into the sea
And the black waves devour him
As if the whole sea were leviathan
But whoever takes to the sea must go with the wind
Seas and shores are the homes of wind

The sea and its wind are the sailor's problems
He weighs anchor and leaves port
He knows the wind and the currents
Or he will not reach home

With the sea there is wind
With men there is struggle
The struggles of men are the artist's problems
He must know men and their history
They are his means of creation
Show the audience the solution
But show them the problem
Make the problem fruitful!